A dance through time

A dance through time

IMAGES OF WESTERN SOCIAL DANCING
FROM THE MIDDLE AGES TO MODERN TIMES

JEREMY BARLOW

Bodleian Library
UNIVERSITY OF OXFORD

First published in 2012 by
the Bodleian Library
Broad Street
Oxford OX1 3BG

www.bodleianbookshop.co.uk

ISBN 978 1 85124 299 3

Text © Jeremy Barlow, 2012

All images, unless specified, are © Bodleian Library,
University of Oxford, 2012.

Cover design by Dot Little
Designed and typeset by illuminati, Grosmont
in 11½ on 16 Monotype Baskerville and Champignon
Printed and bound by Great Wall Printing, China
on Go Ching 157 gsm matt art paper

British Library Catalogue in Publishing Data
A CIP record of this publication
is available from the British Library

Contents

To friends and colleagues in dance, through time

Introduction

As a teenager in the 1950s, I was sent off to dancing
lessons and learnt, or tried to learn, the waltz,
the quickstep, a sanitized jive and the easier Latin
American dances, just before they were swept away by
rock'n'roll. The lessons seemed a duty rather than a
pleasure; another middle-class exercise in acquiring a
behavioural code that inhibited expression of feeling.
Half a century later, sifting through hundreds of
images of social dance for this book, it became apparent that the contrast between those lessons and the
untutored vitality of rock'n'roll marked the end of a
centuries-old tension between decorum and licence on
the dance floor. That tension permeates much of the
book.

 The first two chapters, 'Poised in Performance'
and 'Symbolic Circles', investigate the challenges for
an artist in conveying a sense of movement through
a frozen moment, and for the viewer in drawing
conclusions about the realism or artificiality of the
resulting image. 'Decorous Dance' focuses on dancing
in which flamboyant gesture is limited; artists have
found it harder to create a sense of movement when
feet remain close to the ground and arm movement is restricted or formalized. In 'Illustrations
for Instruction' the images relate to the teaching of
such dances. The remaining three chapters illustrate
breaches of decorum, in terms of morals, class and

manners. Expression of sexual attraction through dance has always threatened propriety: the images in 'Dance and Desire' display crude exhibitionism and insinuations of depravity, but also visions of a more romanticized desire. Further threats to propriety have come from those who, for reasons of class, clumsiness or unrestrained enjoyment, do not dance or behave 'properly' according to genteel standards. The chapter 'Rustic Revels' looks at rural dancing in genre prints and drawings from Germany and the Low Countries in the sixteenth to early seventeenth centuries, while 'Burlesquing the Bourgeois' explores humour directed at the middle classes in the nineteenth and early twentieth centuries.

The idea for *A Dance Through Time* came from my previous Bodleian Library publication, *The Cat & the Fiddle: Images of Musical Humour from the Middle Ages to Modern Times*. A number of illustrations there show humans or animals dancing, and it seemed that the diverse and sometimes idiosyncratic Bodleian bequests which contributed to the book might also yield material for a volume on the illustration of Western social dance, covering roughly the same period. As in *The Cat & the Fiddle*, foremost among those bequests are the codices, books, prints and drawings donated by Francis Douce (1757–1834). Dance played a significant part in Douce's fascination with social life and customs, and images selected from his collections span the fifteenth to eighteenth centuries. John Johnson's bequest of ephemera (more than a million items) also contains a proportion of dance-related material, especially from the late eighteenth to the early twentieth centuries. The collection of sheet music donated by Walter Harding includes many dances for piano with illustrated covers from the years either side of 1900.

Douce's prints and drawings were transferred to the Ashmolean Museum in 1915, and I am grateful to the Museum for allowing images from other bequests too to be incorporated. I must also thank *Dancing Times*, Carlton Books, Getty Images, dance artist Brenda Naylor and cartoonist Dan Piraro for permission to use images that take the book through to the twenty-first century. A number of dance historians have given valuable advice, including Françoise Carter, Anne Daye, Moira Goff, Ann and Paul Kent, Margaret McGowan, Christine and Ellis Rogers, and Jennifer Thorp. Remaining inaccuracies and misconceptions are my responsibility. I am grateful to Clover Peake and M.A. Stewart for help with Latin and Greek translations, to Melanie Florence for help with the medieval French of *The Romance of Alexander*, and to Alison Stewart and Andrew Edmunds for advice on prints. Mollie Webb, Librarian at the Imperial Society of Teachers of Dancing, has been most helpful.

Finally I must thank editors Deborah Susman and Janet Phillips for their patience over the long time it has taken to complete the book.

ONE
Poised in performance

Seven hundred years separate the performers in (1) and (2), yet their mid-action poses have features in common that lead us to assume they are dancing. The raised, bent knee especially has acted as a pictogram for dance over millennia; an Egyptian hieroglyph for dance consisted of a stick figure with one knee raised.[1]

The illustrators have not provided any setting for the performances. The dancers' positions in relation to the ground cannot be inferred from, for example, a foot shadow or patterned floor. As a result they seem to be airborne, although the straight right foot of the man on the right in (1) may lead interpretive instinct, conditioned by classical ballet, to imagine that his right foot toe touches the ground. His mouth is open as if speaking or singing, while the woman on the left looks more acrobatic, as if leaping over an object. Both figures gesture with their arms, mimetically perhaps. The distinctions of genre we make between dance, acrobatics, mime and song today did not necessarily apply in the late thirteenth century. In any case we do not know to what extent the illustration reflected performance practice or the wishes of a

1. TWO DANCERS. Late-thirteenth-century Bible, England. The illumination appears on the first page of the Book of Isaiah; a historiated capital at the start shows a man looking with raised hand at the walls of a city (Jerusalem?) with gates open.

patron; further information is needed. Dance artist Brenda Naylor confirms that the youth she sketched in (2) is dancing, but the Old Testament text above the figures in (1) – the start of Isaiah – does not mention dance. For Christians, the Book of Isaiah contains passages that prefigure the coming of Christ, so are the figures literally dancing for joy? One of the hieroglyphs for dance can, in conjunction with other hieroglyphs, signify joy. Images of dance may carry symbolic meanings that skew realistic interpretation, as we shall see in the next chapter. Here, any attempt to link image and text, realistically or symbolically, remains speculative.

In the Middle Ages, illustrations and written accounts portray dance, at all levels of society, as primarily an outdoor activity, though performances in churches, taverns and halls are recorded. When, in the Renaissance, dance among the higher social ranks moved indoors onto smoother surfaces, footwork close to the floor became the decorous ideal. The raised, sharply bent knee – as in the current expression 'a knees-up' – now often signified dance that violated decorum. Rustic dancers in (3) perform outdoors with

angular knees and elbows on a rough surface that demands raised feet; the noble dancers above have straight or gently curved limbs and footwork keeps closer to the ground on a smooth, presumably interior floor. The rustic dancers perform more energetically than their noble counterparts;

2. HIP HOPPER. Brenda Naylor, 1999. The artist made numerous sketches during workshops at the summer series Ballroom Blitz, held at London's South Bank Centre during the 1990s.

5

a swirling skirt rises to reveal the legs of the second woman from the left. Polite society considered such display unseemly, though genteel dancers did behave flamboyantly on occasion: 'In voltas and other similarly lascivious and unruly dances now fashionable … young women have to leap in such a way that they often show their bare knees' wrote dance instructor Thoinot Arbeau in the treatise *Orchésographie* (1588). His pupil Capriol, an aspiring young gentleman, replies: 'This way of dancing seems to me neither beautiful nor decent, except for dancing with some lusty serving wench.'[2] Most comment on dance in the Renaissance comes from a male perspective.

The artist has caught many of the rustic dancers off balance, at an angle to the vertical, whereas the noble dancers carry themselves with upright, composed

Hîc púdor, hîc morum probitas hîc aúlica suada,   *Et h*

Qúantúm aúla à Caúla : tantúm quoq̃ distat agresti   *Aulicus : hoc præsens*

de Bríj fe. et excud:

de Bríj fe.

bearing. Latin texts (freely translated) reinforce the distinctions of rank: 'Here there is honour, integrity and courtly influence; charm, nobility and moderation flourish. What a surprise, seeing that divine attributes follow the gods'; this description contrasts with its counterpart, 'The peasant is as remote from the courtier as the sheepcote from the palace: the unruly dancing here will teach you as much. But that's fine; such are the differences in varied lives.'

Contrasts of social rank extend to the music. Musicians accompanying the rustics play a raucous shawm (ancestor of the oboe) and bagpipe, instruments that carry well outdoors; the bagpipe in particular had rustic associations (see (9), (37), (38) and (39)). The noble dancers perform to quieter instruments, appropriate to an indoor environment: two fiddles,

3. COURTLY AND RUSTIC DANCERS. Théodore de Bry (1528–1598), c. 1550. This pair of prints has been reproduced in several books on dance history, to demonstrate the contrasting dance styles of court and country.

s vitæ generosa modeſtia gliſcit. *Quid mirúm, divas vltrò ſi diâ ſequantúr.*

a Chorea docebit. *Sed bene, ſic variæ liqueant diſcrimina vitæ.*

Plate II.

Designed, Engraved, and Publish'd by Wm. Hogarth, March 5th 1753, according to Act of Parliament.

4. THE COUNTRY DANCE. William Hogarth (1697–1764), 1753. The print belongs to Hogarth's treatise on aesthetics *The Analysis of Beauty*; it was also sold separately. Hogarth used the marginal images to explain his principle about beauty as a property of curved lines that are neither too straight nor too angular. Note, top left, the floor patterns of the country dance and of a couple dance immediately beneath.

bass viol and lute. The latter combination occurs, with slight variations, in many indoor dance scenes over the following 250 years (see (5), (19) and (20)).

Even the engraving styles of the two strips differ. The rustic dancers have been etched boldly, with long, deep lines that accentuate movement in skirts and clothing, whereas the courtly dancers are engraved more delicately. The difference is so marked that one wonders if the two strips were made by the same engraver. The rustic dancers are similar in character to those in the German engraver Sebald Beham's *Das Bauernfest oder die zwölf Monate* (The Peasant Festival or the Twelve Months) series of prints (1546); Beham did not illustrate noble dance. Both sets of de Bry's dancers are replicated in a much larger series of woodcuts by the Swiss artist Tobias Stimmer. It is not known who copied whom. Beham learnt from Albrecht Dürer, whose engraving *Peasant Couple Dancing* (1514) may have been a common source of influence on Beham, de Bry and later illustrators of rustic dance (see Chapter 6). The only conduct shared in de Bry's two strips comes from the noble couple furthest to the left and the rustic pair second from the right; both are locked in a face-to-face hold not generally approved in genteel dance until the nineteenth century, after the advent of waltzing. The remaining noble couples demonstrate the side-by-side position that was the norm.

Two centuries after de Bry, William Hogarth displayed contrasts of decorum within a single print and a restricted range of social rank (4). The 'genteel turns'[3] of the couple to the left present a grace and elegance at odds with the clumsiness or gawky pretensions of the remaining five couples; all partake in a country dance. Hogarth used the print to demonstrate

an aesthetic principle. It was sold with his treatise
The Analysis of Beauty (1753), in which he tried to
establish an empirical basis for beauty, divorced from
moral judgement. Central to his thesis is a 'line of
beauty' – an elongated *S* – which, if it is too straight,
becomes 'mean and poor', or too curvaceous, 'gross
and clumsy'.[4] Hogarth saw the line of beauty in
floor patterns of a minuet and country dance, in the
undulating rise and fall of dancers as they progress,
and in the comportment of their body and limbs. But
he warned of dangers in attempting to illustrate dance:

> The best representation in a picture, of even the most
> elegant dancing, as every figure is rather a suspended
> action in it rather than an attitude, must be always
> somewhat unnatural and ridiculous; for were it possible
> in a real dance to fix every person at one instant of
> time, as in a picture, not one in twenty would appear
> to be graceful, tho' each were ever so much so in their
> movements; nor could the figure of the dance itself be at
> all understood.[5]

Avoidance of the 'unnatural and ridiculous' in
illustrations of decorous dance often results in figures
that do not look much as if they are dancing. At first
sight, we might assume that the seventeenth-century
French couple in (5) are simply walking down the
room towards us in a rather affected manner. But the
typical dance band in the background – two fiddles
and a bass violin or cello – and the verses beneath
leave us in no doubt. The second verse translates:

> Each in their turn they enter the ball
> To the sound of the violins which give the tempo.
> One looks closely to see who dances best
> With most grace, or who performs badly.

From the early Renaissance up to the advent of
the waltz, one couple at a time performed to the

Le Blond excud auec Priuilege du Roy

Le Blond excud auec Priuilege du Roy

Qui ne defireroit eftre tout couuert d'yeux:
Pour bien confiderer les beautez de ces Dames
Qui parent cé Balet: leurs regards et leurs flames
Peuuent vaincre les cueurs des hommes et des dieux.

Chacunes a leur tour elles entrent au Bal
Au fon des violons qui donnent la cadence.
L'oeil obferue attentif celle qui le mieux dance
Auecque plus de grace: ou celle qui faict mal.

C'eft en
Rauiffe
Ou Ven
Content

...lec ou les diuers plaisirs
...la vûe, et les oreilles,
...nt, ou les bouches vermeilles
...ans librement leur desirs.

Si l'Amour quelque part bastit son Paradis,
C'est ou l'on faict Balet, on y void faces d'Anges
Au lieu d'Astres la joye y est dans les meslanges
D'Ebats et passetemps plus grands qui ne sont dits.

5. LE BAL. Jean Le Blond (c. 1590–1666), c. 1635, after a design by Abraham Bosse (c. 1603–1676). Many copies of this print survive and, as with the prints in (3), it has been reproduced frequently.

assembled company for a good part of the ball (there were exceptions to this practice, as will be seen). Guests were both participants and spectators. Dance was an essential social grace; the way you danced informed your bearing and behaviour generally (see p. 46). As a dancer you were on display and your performance needed practice and rehearsal.

Oddly enough, the competitive element in Renaissance and baroque social dance has revived via the medium of television. In 1949 the BBC initiated its series *Come Dancing* with broadcasts from dance studios around Britain, and the programme became competitive from 1953. Although dances current in 1949 – the waltz, foxtrot, quickstep and Latin American dances – were obsolete for most by the early 1960s, they remained embedded in *Come Dancing* to the end of the series in 1998 and continued to be performed when

6. POSITION IN THE CHA-CHA-CHA. From Peggy Spencer's *The Joy of Dancing: The Next Steps* (Carlton Books, 1999).

a revamped version involving celebrities, *Strictly Come Dancing*, was launched in 2004.

Interest in twentieth-century ballroom dances stimulated by the programmes has resulted in a number of publications, including Peggy Spencer's teach-yourself books *The Joy of Dancing* (1997 and 1999). The similar comportment of the couples in (5) and (6) shows how certain ideals of decorum have remained consistent over the centuries, even if the dances themselves are quite different. The two images also demonstrate the danger of trying to name a dance from a frozen moment; who would guess that the couple in (6) are demonstrating part of a phrase in the lively Latin American cha-cha-cha? All thirty-three photographs in *The Joy of Dancing* that illustrate progressions and variations in the cha-cha-cha show the pair with feet touching the ground, whereas a photo of the dance mid-performance (7) captures each dancer with one foot raised in a 'knees-up' position. The two images, incidentally, demonstrate respectively Hogarth's distinction between 'attitude' and 'suspended action'. To identify a dance from an illustration, characteristic features need to be present; for example, one can be reasonably certain that the dances in (20) and (21) are a minuet and allemande respectively.

Any visual image of social dance, moving or still, transforms an activity enjoyed by the performer into a display for the viewer. Illustrators or photographers inevitably create a 'staged' effect as they frame their captured instant and will

7. COUPLE PERFORMING THE CHA-CHA-CHA. From Peggy Spencer's *The Joy of Dancing: The Next Steps* (Carlton Books, 1999).

often go for the eye-catching extreme position of a movement: a knee raised, arms outstretched, the high point of a leap. They also bring their own cultural baggage, with its expectations and biases, to their portrayals (as will those, including myself, who select images to illustrate an argument or theme). 'The observer inevitably conditions our view of the dance' writes dance historian Margaret McGowan.[6] Furthermore, if dancers know they are being watched, then they may, even unintentionally, change the way they dance for the onlooker. The so-called 'observer effect' comes into play, whereby the presence of an onlooker alters the custom or practice being watched. An example of the phenomenon takes place in (8), where a dancer has noticed the photographer and performs in a way that she probably would not have done had he not been there.

The images so far have highlighted some of the factors involved in representing and interpreting a frozen moment of dance: the use of illustrative formulas and stereotypical portrayals; the framing and choice of scene; the perspective and cultural background of artist and viewer, and the effect of the artist's presence. The possibility of symbolic meaning has been touched on, and the next chapter explores this element further, with particular reference to circle dances.

8. ROBERT AND MARGUERITE O'HARA. The photograph has on the back 'International 1967. Robert and Margeruite [sic] O'Hara.' That year, for the third time, the couple won the Professional Champions title for England in the International Latin American Dance Championships.

TWO

Symbolic circles

At midnight on New Year's Eve we stand in a circle, hold hands with arms crossed and sing 'Auld Lang Syne' while moving our arms in time to the song. We're aware that this static dance celebrates the arrival of the new year; perhaps also that joining hands relates to the theme of remembered and enduring friendship in Burns's lyrics.

Circle dances often have a significance beyond the physical act. It takes two to tango, but when three or more join hands to dance, they experience a communality distinct from the one-to-one intimacy of a couple dance. Yet in drawing the participants together for celebration, the circle at the same time excludes the observer, who may construe the performance as secret, mystical, ritualistic. The symbolism of the circle as a shape – representing unity, perfection, eternity and much else – has, over millennia, further imbued the circle dance with additional meaning.

Plato, in the fourth century BCE, viewed the sun, moon, planets and stars as deities that orbited the earth in a complex relationship: 'To describe all the figures of these gods, circling in a dance, would be labour spent in vain.'[7] The notion of a cosmic dance, however far-fetched today, persisted through the Middle Ages and Renaissance. The dance instruction book *Orchésographie* (1588), mentioned in the previous chapter, concludes with the advice: 'Practise these dances properly and you will be a companion of the planets, which dance naturally.'⁸ But the circle dance has been endowed with special significance in many other contexts too. The author of the apocryphal Acts of St John replaced the Last Supper of the Gospels with the following description:

> He [Jesus] bade us therefore make as it were a ring, holding one another's hands, and himself standing in the midst he said: Answer Amen unto me. He began, then, to sing an hymn and to say: Glory be to thee, Father. And we, going about in a ring, answered him: Amen.⁹

Geoffrey of Monmouth, medieval chronicler of British history, described Stonehenge and its circular layout as a *chorea gigantum*¹⁰ (dance of giants) in his *Historia Regum Britanniae* (1135–38). For Shakespeare, the circle dance played a part in evoking the magical, supernatural worlds of fairies and witches. In *A Midsummer Night's Dream*, Titania, queen of the fairies, summons a 'roundel' and song from her fairy train (2.ii); near the end of *The Merry Wives of Windsor*, humans disguised as fairies frighten Falstaff and dance around him (5.v); in *Macbeth*, three witches dance and chant in a ring as Macbeth and Banquo first enter (1.iii).

During the nineteenth century European explorers, missionaries and colonizers reported circle dances in many parts of the world. The dances and those who performed them were often described as 'primitive'; the adjective, originally meaning much the same as 'ancient', became applied to peoples considered less developed in thought and culture than the Europeans who encountered them. Now seen as primitive, ancient and universal, the circle dance provided a convenient starting point for narratives of dance history. Take for

9. NATIVITY SCENE AND SHEPHERDS' DANCE. By the Master of Gijsbrecht van Brederode. Book of Hours, Utrecht, c.1460–65. The historiated *D* as the first letter of *Deus*, top left, shows the Nativity: Mary and Joseph worship the baby Jesus. At the bottom shepherds have thrown down their staves to dance in celebration. The little trowels on the ends of the staves occur in other medieval images of shepherds. They were used to scoop up and throw earth or stones as a means of controlling the sheep. Musical accompaniment is suggested by a bagpiper playing to the left of the dancers, while another plays in the right-hand margin.

example two formerly influential works: *Dancing* (1895) by Lilly Grove and *World History of the Dance* (1937) by Curt Sachs. *Dancing* opens with 'The Dances of Antiquity', where Grove asserts that 'most primitive dances were certainly circular'. In her next chapter, titled 'The Dances of Savages', she compares dances performed for magical purposes around a central object or figure in various cultures. Grove often quotes her husband Sir James Frazer, who in *The Golden Bough* (1890) proposed an evolution of human belief and thought that begins with magic, progresses to religion and finally to science. In *A World History of Dance* Curt Sachs goes one stage further than Grove by claiming that the circle dance could be traced back not just to 'primitive man', but to his evolutionary forebears, the apes. To support his proposition he tendentiously re-phrases a passage from Wolfgang Köhler's *The Mentality of Apes* (1925) which describes dance-like behaviour in chimpanzees; Köhler had spent several years studying a colony of chimpanzees on Tenerife. In Köhler, the chimpanzees 'appear full of eager enjoyment of their primitive game'; for Sachs they 'appear to take a keen delight in this primitive round dance'. An 'approximate rhythm' in Köhler becomes a 'distinct rhythm' in Sachs. Köhler places the word 'dance' in quotation marks; Sachs does not. Sachs also ignores a sentence that strongly suggests human influence on the captive chimpanzees' behaviour; Köhler writes how a 'trusted human friend' of the chimpanzees instigated rhythmic foot stamping and the circling of a post.[11]

Such perceptions of the circle dance fed into twentieth-century reaction against romanticism in the visual and performing arts; examples include Matisse's painting *La danse* (The Dance) (two versions, 1909 and 1910), Debussy's score *Rondes de printemps* (Round

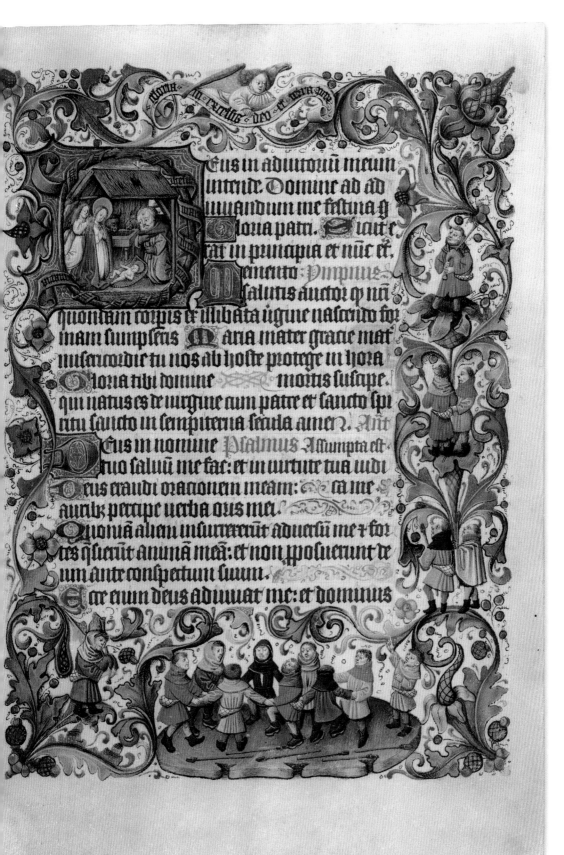

eus in adiutoriu meum
intende. Domine ad ad
iuuandum me festina. g
loria patri. Sicut e
rat in principio et nuc et.
Memento. Virginis
salutis auctor qp nri
quoniam corpis et illibata uirgine nascendo for
mam sumpseris Maria mater gracie mat
misericordie tu nos ab hoste protege in hora
Gloria tibi domine mortis suscipe.
qui natus es de uirgine cum patre et sancto spi
ritu sancto in sempiterna secula amen. Ant
Eus in nomine Psalmus Assumpta est
tuo saluum me fac: et in uirtute tua iudi
Deus exaudi oracionem meam: ca me
auribz percipe uerba oris mei.
Quoniam alieni insurrexerunt aduersum me et for
tes quesierunt animam meam: et non proposuerunt de
um ante conspectum suum.
Ecce enim deus adiuuat me: et dominus

Dances of Spring) (1909) from *Images pour orchestra* (Orchestral Images) and Stravinsky's ballet *Le sacre du printemps* (The Rite of Spring) (1913). Stravinsky wrote that the ballet grew from his vision of 'a solemn pagan rite: sage elders, seated in a circle, watched a young girl – the Chosen One – dance herself to death. They were sacrificing her to propitiate the god of spring.'[12] The lead-up to the final sacrifice includes a section 'Cercles mystérieux des adolescentes' (Mystic Circles of the Young Girls).

Artists and illustrators have, over the centuries, exploited and developed the many meanings given to circle dances. The examples that follow range chronologically from the mid-fifteenth to mid-twentieth centuries. In (9) the illuminator has embellished the Nativity story with a *bas de page* of shepherds dancing in celebration. Notice how one of the shepherds at the front of the circle faces sideways rather than inwards. This illustrative device – found in images throughout the chapter – avoids a uniform view of the foremost dancers' backs, but sometimes creates an awkward or impossible moment of performance. The sideways-facing shepherd has an additional purpose: in stepping to the left he demonstrates the clockwise progression of the dance. Superstition attaches to the direction of circular motions generally, from passing the port to stirring a pot. Clockwise movement (sunwise, or in the direction of the sun) is considered proper, propitious and Christian; proceeding anticlockwise (widdershins) brings bad luck and evil.

In (10) the central figure at the front faces right. Although he confronts a left-facing figure, three of the four dancers proceed widdershins. The gruesome semi-skeletons, their gaping stomachs crawling with worms, take after woodcuts in *Danse macabre* (Dance

10. DANCE OF DEATH. Book of Hours, France, 1525–50. The illustration is one of several in the volume that show figures of death confronting ecclesiastics and other dignitaries on opposite pages, following the theme of Marchant's *Danse macabre*. A king stands to the right of the dancers in the margin of this page.

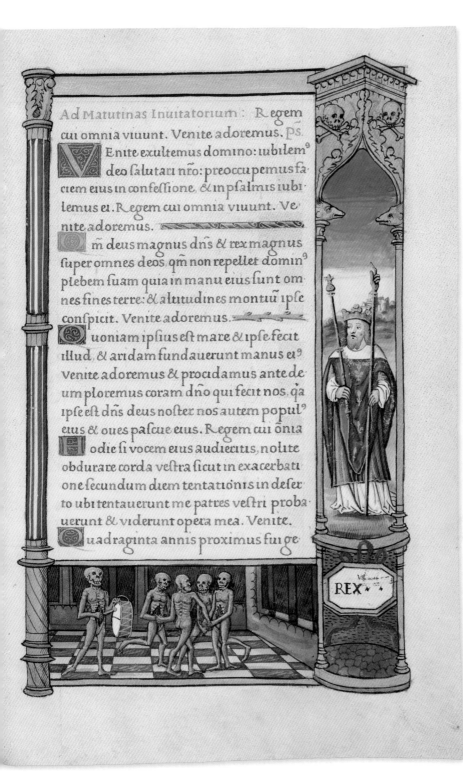

Ad Matutinas Inuitatorium : Regem
cui omnia viuunt. Venite adoremus. ps.

Enite exultemus domino: iubilem⁹
deo salutati nⁱo: preoccupemus fa
ciem eius in confessione, & in psalmis iubi
lemus ei. Regem cui omnia viuunt. Ve
nite adoremus.

m deus magnus dñs & rex magnus
super omnes deos, qm non repellet domin⁹
plebem suam quia in manu eius sunt om
nes fines terre: & altitudines montiũ ipse
conspicit. Venite adoremus.

uoniam ipsius est mare & ipse fecit
illud, & aridam fundauerunt manus ei⁹
Venite adoremus & procidamus ante de
um ploremus coram dño qui fecit nos, qa
ipse est dñs deus noster nos autem popul⁹
eius & oues pascue eius. Regem cui ōnia

odie si vocem eius audieritis, nolite
obdurare corda vestra sicut in exacerbati
one secundum diem tentatiōnis in deser
to ubi tentauerunt me patres vestri proba
uerunt & viderunt opera mea. Venite.

uadraginta annis proximus fui ge

REX

of Death), a best-seller published in 1485 by the Parisian printer Guyot Marchant. The book's text and, probably, illustrations derive in turn from the earliest known *Danse macabre*, a series of images and verses painted on a wall at the Cimetière des Innocents, Paris, in 1425 (the wall was knocked down in 1669). The poem and illustrations in Marchant's book do not portray an actual dance, but constitute a procession that starts with pope and emperor, and then descends through the hierarchy of church and state to the lowest and poorest: parson and labourer, clerk and hermit, friar minor and child. The characters are shown with corresponding figures of death that often display open, worm-ridden stomachs and are not fully skeletal; they represent the rotting corpses of those they accompany. The moral is that 'Death spareth not low nor high degree; [neither] Popes, Kings, nor worthy Emperors.'[13] Fully skeletal figures of death first made their appearance with the publication of Hans Holbein's *Danse macabre* engravings in 1538.

The dancers, objects and text in (11) invite a search for meaning. Headed *Chorea Mundi* (Dance of the World), it concerns in overall theme the folly and deception of worldly ambition, as encapsulated in the Latin word *vanitas* inscribed on the bale of hay below the central figure. It translates as emptiness, vanity, boasting, inconstancy, falsehood, pride, ambition, flattery. *Vanitas* also describes a type of Flemish and Dutch still-life painting from Vrints's time, containing objects that symbolize the impermanence of our existence, such as a skull, clock or hourglass. Although these are not present here, other symbols from *vanitas* paintings may be seen. For example, the jug on its side stands for emptiness; the crown on the bale of hay and the orb and sceptre on the woman's head represent power and worldly possessions, and the hay itself symbolizes the transience of human life. The woman at the centre probably represents Lady World, 'an allegorical representation of evil in the world, whereby the "world" is regarded as a female deceiver and seductress'.[14] However, the inclusion of emblematic objects or figures does not necessarily mean that an artist had a single answer, or any answer, as to their significance; 'they are not necessarily proof of conscious allegorizing on the part of the artist; they may indicate no more than the existence of a traditional repertoire of objects on which he was accustomed to draw.'[15]

The male performers do not hold hands as they circle the woman; each is out for himself as he tries to attract her attention. Sharply bent knees and angular posture denote exhibitionism and lack of decorum. They progress anticlockwise, or widdershins. A moralistic verse beneath the print reinforces *vanitas* in all its meanings, with a warning against 'the falseness which seems beautiful, which seems to flatter you'.

For all its artificiality, Vrints's print actually derives from a real dance, usually performed by men and known as the *moresca*, or by cognate terms including 'morris' in Britain (it is the ancestor of today's folk dance). Described in records of European court entertainments from the mid-1400s, the exhibitionistic display might have included 'high leaping, fighting, mimed action, individual rather than concerted or figured action, dancing in a circle or around the room, rhythmic stepping, beating time with implements, and the use of dancing bells'.[16] Some performances incorporated a woman and a Fool; the men competed for the woman's attention and the Fool eventually won her, or the prize she offered. Here

11. CHOREA MUNDI. (*overleaf*) Johannes Baptista Vrints (1552–1612), n.d.. Vrints is known as a print publisher rather than as a designer; here he gives his own name, but not that of the designer. The musician plays a bladder pipe, in which the inflated bladder provides a reservoir of air to produce a continuous sound, as with the bagpipe. A fiddle, more appropriate to the indoor environment, sticks out of the player's pocket. The coarser, strident sound of the bladder pipe acts as aural mockery, 'blowing a raspberry' at the performers.

25

DEN DANS DES WERELTS

LEX

VANITAS

Joan. Baptista Vrints exc.

the Fool emerges, holding a mask, from the gown of the Lady World figure. The prize she offers is a piece of fruit. An example of a Fool winning the woman in competition with other dancers – though they do not dance in a circle – occurs at a lower social level in *The Wooing of Nan*, an English stage jig for the public theatre of Vrints's time (jigs were a sung, danced and mimed entertainment performed after the main play). A hundred years earlier the Scottish poet William Dunbar had satirized competitive dancing among courtiers in his scatological 'Of a Dance in the Quenis Chalmer [Queen's Chamber]';[17] seven dancers, including two women and Dunbar himself, strive in turn to make an impression. Apart from one of the women they all disgrace themselves through incontinence.

Four of Vrints's performers wear bells, a feature of the English Morris. The custom was not exclusive to the *moresca* in the Renaissance; the French author Antonius Arena, in his Rabelaisian dance treatise *Ad suos Compagniones Studiantes* (To His Student Companions) (1529), implied that dancers with bells performed in different types of entertainment: 'On the last day of Carnival, do the sprightly morescas, and farces too, and also mummeries.... And, I beg you, foot the rhythm correctly; to the jingle of pellet bells.'[18]

The classical imagery in (12) has no basis in reality; it simply indicates the elevated nature of a ball at London's Mansion House. The sumptuously decorated Palladian building, built in the mid-eighteenth century as official residence of the annually elected Lord Mayor, incorporates a splendid ballroom. The engraving on the invitation card shows four scantily draped boys moving gracefully sunwise. To their left a garlanded figure holds a goblet aloft and provides a

12. INVITATION CARD FOR
A BALL AT THE MANSION
HOUSE, 11 APRIL 1814.
Designed by Henry Corbould
(1787–1844). Two months
after the ball, Lord Mayor
William Domville presided at
a Guildhall banquet given by
the Corporation of London
for the Prince Regent and
the Allied Sovereigns. The
occasion cost almost £25,000
(about £1.5 million today) and
shortly after Domville was
created baronet.

hint of Bacchic revelry; perhaps the occasion, though
decorous, will be festive too. The aulos providing the
music has a double significance. It was the instrument
of Euterpe, muse of music and lyric poetry, but also
of the satyrs that attended Bacchus. Henry Corbould,
who designed the image, developed an early taste
for classical subjects and later spent thirty years at
the British Museum making drawings of the Elgin
Marbles and other Greek antiquities.

While Corbould portrays a scene of classical in-
nocence, Thomas Stothard, working during the same
period, takes us into the world of romantic desire (13).
Stothard, like Corbould, had a successful career as

29

13. DANCERS IN A
LANDSCAPE. Thomas
Stothard (1755–1834), Pen and
watercolour, n.d.. The sketch
formed part of a collection
of Stothard drawings that
included an autograph letter
dated 1824 to the printmaker
and antiquary J.T. Smith.
The collection was amassed
by the painter Sir August
Wall Callcott for his wife,
author and art critic Maria
Callcott. She considered
Stothard to be 'the English
Botticelli'.

an illustrator, but he also achieved distinction as a
history painter and left a small fortune at his death.
In this watercolour sketch Stothard shows seven
women dancing widdershins (a hint of paganism?) in a
woodland glade, accompanied by flute and tambour. A
young man's passion for one of the dancers disrupts the
flow, while her partner drags her back into the mo-
mentum of the dance. Torn between opposing forces,
the young woman holds an anatomically impossible
pose, suggesting that the sketch was made quickly. Her
limbs, just visible through a gauzy dress, proceed to
the right, yet either her torso or head twist through 180
degrees as she faces the man she almost kisses.

No text relating to the sketch survives, but one can make conjectural links to Stothard's other work in the early 1820s. Like a number of artists, he produced paintings based on Keats's poems after the latter's death in 1821, and the frozen moment of almost kissing evokes the poet's lines on two lovers in 'Ode on a Grecian Urn':

> Bold Lover, never, never canst thou kiss,
> Though winning near the goal – yet, do not grieve;
> She cannot fade, though thou hast not thy bliss,
> For ever wilt thou love, and she be fair![19]

The sketch also resembles one of the prints Stothard designed for an edition of Boccaccio's *Decameron* published in 1825. The prints do not illustrate Boccaccio's tales, as recounted in idyllic surroundings by ten rich young Florentines escaping from the plague; instead they relate to interludes between the ten days of storytelling. In the evening of the seventh day, the companions wander by a lake and among trees in the grounds of a palace. A couple sing a duet and then all join in *caroles* (the term often described a circle dance), accompanied with instruments. Stothard's print for the scene, like his sketch, shows a woodland setting with dancers accompanied by a tambour player and a flautist. But instead of a *carole*, two couples dance and four young women look on. If the sketch formed an initial concept for the print, then the atmosphere of passionate desire might have been sparked by lines from a song of unrequited love that one of the young women, Filomena, sings to her friends after they have danced:

> If I perchance should hold thee once again,
> I may not be the fool
> That I have been before to let thee go.
> My grasp this time I firmer will maintain;

THE MAY POLE

HANHART LITH.

JUVENILE QUADRILLE,
ON POPULAR ENGLISH MELODIES
ARRANGED BY,

JULES ROCHARD.

Ent. Sta. Hall.   Price 4/~

DUFF & STEWART 2 HANOVER ST.

JUST PUBLISHED LOVE'S YOUNG DREAM. JUVENILE QUADRILLE ON IRISH MELODIES. 4/~
THE WEE BAIRNIES JUVENILE QUADRILLE ON SCOTCH MELODIES .... 4/~

Let fate do what she will,
For I must satisfy my craving soul
With thy sweet lips[20]

If interpretation of Stothard's mysterious dancers remains conjectural, then a sheet music cover from the second half of the nineteenth century showing an English maypole dance (14) must surely have a basis in reality. In fact, the illustrator has created a scene that incorporates much wishful thinking. May games and maypole dances declined in the early years of the century, but were revived with increasing force from the 1830s as part of a 'Merrie England' reinvention of rural traditions. The landed gentry who initiated the revivals introduced new elements into May games, including the replacement of young men and women by children for maypole dances. The music here is for a 'Juvenile Quadrille', and the cover shows children dancing round the pole while the gentry look on approvingly. Children and adults are dressed in a Victorian conception of eighteenth-century clothes; the scene presents an idealized Arcadian past, when all classes of rural society lived in harmony. The two foremost dancers face outwards, holding a balletic posture that makes the direction of the dance unclear. The boys either side face inwards, creating an im- plausible choreographic moment. Tennyson caught the mood of nostalgia for May games in his poem 'The May Queen' (1832), which describes the excitement of a young woman who wins the title. By the end of the year she is dying and recollects her moment of glory:

Last May we made a crown of flowers: we had a
    merry day;
Beneath the hawthorn on the green they made me
    Queen of May;
And we danced about the may-pole and in the hazel
    copse,

14. THE MAY POLE, n.d. The illustrator has attempted a quintessentially English scene – the music is based on 'popular English melodies' – but the large house in the background with oversized eves looks decidedly continental. The distinguished lithographers M. & N. Hanhart, who produced the print (signed bottom left), operated in London, but the artist is not known.

Till Charles's Wain came out above the tall white
chimney-tops.[21]

Before the nineteenth-century revival, maypole
dances were not always circular. Although expressions
such as 'dancing about the maypole' occur in early
documents, 'about' may mean 'in the vicinity of'
rather than the forming of a circle.

Discussion of the maypole's significance reveals that
interpretations of traditional rites by outsiders may not
be shared by those who participate. The maypole has
been viewed as a phallic symbol, a divine tree and,
by Sir James Frazer, as a tree spirit bestowing fertility.
Ronald Hutton has written that there is no evidence
that people involved with the maypole in Europe
viewed it in such ways: 'the poles, like the fetching
of green branches, were simply signs that the happy
season of warmth and comfort had returned. They
were useful frameworks upon which garlands and
other decoration could be hung, to form a focal point
for celebration'.[22]

Finally, a photograph (15) of a circle dance that
needs no decoding or interpretation. On 8 May 1945
Londoners took to the streets after Winston Churchill
had announced the end of the Second World War in
Europe and declared a national holiday. For performers and onlookers alike the dance simply manifested
celebration and joy. One might conclude with Curt
Sachs that dancing in a circle is an embedded
instinct. But we do not know if the circle formed
spontaneously, if the photographer or anyone else
played a part in staging the scene, or if memories of
Auld Lang Syne and maypole festivities stimulated the
idea of the dance. Newsreel of the celebrations shows
revellers in Trafalgar Square dancing the conga in
a line formation. The most one can say is that when

15. VE (VICTORY IN EUROPE)
DAY. Dancing in Piccadilly
Circus, 8 May 1945. Regent
Street curves round to the
north in the background.

all unite in celebration, then the act of linking and
moving together, whether in a line or a circle, power-
fully expresses communal joy.

THREE

Decorous dance

No sense of joy enlivens the glum, passive figures linking hands for a circular *carole* in (16), even though the occasion is a *graunt feste & revel* (great celebration and entertainment) and the text describes the performers singing *hautement* (strongly) as they perform; it was common practice to sing while dancing a *carole*. But chivalric men and women do not smile or open their mouths in any of the illuminations that accompany this fourteenth-century romance on the adventures

16. *CAROLE*. Workshop of Jehan de Grise, Flanders, 1338–44. From *The Romance of Alexander*. The illustration comes towards the end of 'Le restor du paon' (The Re-creation of the Peacock) by Jehans Brisebare, interpolated into the Alexander romance. In the previous section, 'Les voeux du paon' (The Vows of the Peacock) by Jacques de Longuyon, vows of valour and love are made over the carcass of a peacock following a victory by Alexander's forces. 'Le restor' describes the re-creation of the peacock in bejewelled gold, and celebrations over fifteen days of five marriages; the *carole* is danced on the final day. Vows made to birds were a feature of the chivalric code.

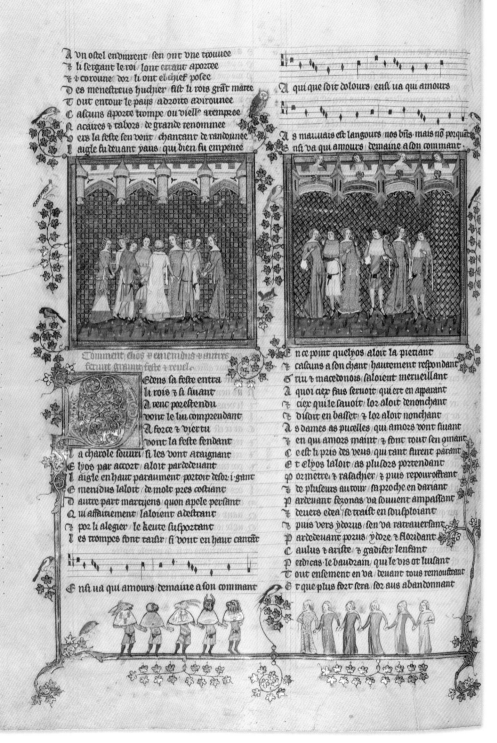

A vn ostel endirent / sen ont vne troulice
⁊ li sergant le roi / lont errant aportee
⁊ ⁊ coroune dor / li ont el chief polee
D es menestrus huchier / fist li rois grāt marèe
T out entour le pays / adroite avirounee
C ascuns aporte trompe / ou vielle atempree
T acaires ⁊ tabors / de grande renomnee
V ers la feste sen vont / chantant de randounee
L aigle fu deuant yaus / qui bien fu empenee

A qui que soit dolours / ensi va qui amours

A s mauuais est langours / nos biēs mais nō porquāt
N si va qui amours / demaine a son commant·

Comment clyos ⁊ enemidus ⁊ autres
seruirt graunt feste ⁊ reuel

E dens sa feste entra
li rois ⁊ li suiant
A venc porestendu
uont le liu comprendant
A force ⁊ viertu
uont la feste fendant
a charole souurt / si les uont Ataignant
E lyos par accort / aloit pardedeuant
L aigle en haut paraument / portoit desoz i gant
E nenidus laloit / de molt pres costiant
D autre part martyens / quon apele persant
Q ui affaitement / laloient adestrant
p or li alegier / le keute susportant
L es trompes sont taisir / si uont en haut cantā

E n ce point quelyos / aloit la pietrant
⁊ cascuns a son chant / hautement respondant
G riu ⁊ macedonois / saloient meruellant
A quoi ciex faus seruoit / qui ert en aparant
⁊ ciex quile sauoit / lor aloit denonchant
⁊ disoit en basset / ⁊ lor aloit nonchant
A s dames as pucelles / qui amors vont suiant
E n qui amors maint / ⁊ sont tout sen ginant
C est li pris des veus / qui tant furent parant
E t elyos laloit / as pludos portendant
qo or mettre ⁊ rasachier / ⁊ puis repouroftrant
⁊ de pluseurs autour / sa proche en dariant
p ardeuant sezonas / va souuent ampassant
⁊ deuers edea / se traist en soulsployant
⁊ puis vers ydorus / sen va ratrauersant
p ardedeuant porzus / ydore ⁊ floridant
C aulus ⁊ ariste / ⁊ gadifer lenfant
p erdicas le baudrain / qui le vis ot luisant
T out ensemble en va / deuant tous remouftrant
E t que plus fort sera / soz aus abandonnant

E nsi va qui amours / demaine a son commant

17. THE *CAROLE* IN CONTEXT. (*previous page*) Workshop of Jehan de Grise, Flanders, 1338–44. From *The Romance of Alexander*. For a transcription of the *carole* tune, see *Sacred & Secular Songs… in the Bodleian Library, Oxford*, ed. Sir John Stainer (London and New York: Novello, 1901), vol. 2, p. 23. In the right-hand panel, men and women gesticulate in a way that suggests conversation, as they do in many other illustrations even though their mouths are always shut. The bird – a hawk – appears elsewhere, and is one of the potential prizes to be awarded for the best vow.

of Alexander the Great. Nine dancers take part, four men and five women; genders alternate, except on the far left where two women stand adjacently. Perhaps we are to imagine the start of the dance; only two figures take a step – anticlockwise, oddly enough – while the rest appear stationary. The illuminator's avoidance of backward-facing dancers in the foreground produces another unlikely positioning for a circle dance; while the centrally placed woman faces inwards and shows her back, the men either side of her face out from the circle. The text describes how the *carole* eventually opens out into a line as the dancers proceed to meet the king and his retinue.

In (17) we see the page that includes the *carole*, with the lyrics – a *rondeau* – and catchy tune that the dancers sing. The words pay tribute to the power of love, regardless of the pain it causes. More dancing takes place along the *bas de page*, where five men in animal masks and six women dance in lines. From their clothes it seems as if at least some of the figures are the same as in the upper panels. The illuminator has given a greater sense of movement to the line dancers; bodies sway sideways. The three 'animals' furthest to the left have the only faces on the page that convey enjoyment; their mouths are open, as if laughing. The masks hide the faces of the noble wearers, perhaps allowing the artist to display their expressions by proxy. The wearing of animal masks occurs in European folk traditions today; an example in England is the Abbots Bromley horn dance. In other countries such annual rites may include frightening, chasing or capturing girls.

The sextet in (18) brings us inside, more than a century and a half later. Dance for higher ranks of society has moved indoors and many images in the

18. SIX DANCERS. Book of Hours, northern France, early sixteenth century. The illumination comes from a section devoted to saints; the text above the dancers praises St Barbara, who is depicted in a panel on the same page.

sixteenth and seventeenth centuries show performers on a floor paved in squares (see, for example, (5), (10) and (19)). As well as reproducing a decorative feature, the pattern serves to locate the dancers spatially. Fifteenth-century Italian treatises name the skilled use of floor space – *compartimento di terreno* – as an attribute essential to achieve perfection in dancing.

Again there is little sense of movement; only the presence of a musician and the positioning of the figures indicate the possibility of dance. Expressions and body language hint at a scenario of male shyness and female impatience. The central man appears defensive, with left arm placed across his stomach.

The man to his left urges him forward physically. The woman in the middle is also being urged forward; she gives a 'why are we waiting' look, casting her eyes heavenwards. To her right, the woman looks exasperated, with one arm akimbo.

One man wears a codpiece instead of a doublet; codpieces had become an essential adornment by the early sixteenth century as doublets were shortened. Arena warned: 'your codpiece must be well tied. We sometimes see codpieces slip to the ground during the bassedanse so you must tie them well.'[23]

The illustration dates from the time of two French dance treatises: Arena's, and the anonymous *S'ensuyvent plusieurs basses dances...* (Here follow several *basses danses*).[24] Both books give choreographies for the *basse danse*, which dominated upper-class social dance in France, and was of major importance in Italy (as the *bassadanza)* and England during the fifteenth and early sixteenth centuries. The stately French *basse danse* had straightforward step sequences and was usually danced by one couple at a time to the assembled company. Arena, however, mentions the practice of a man dancing with two women as something that 'often happens', and he does not approve of several couples crowding the floor, even if 'laws and rules may be broken in some instances'.[25] Fifteenth-century Italian treatises include *bassedanze* choreographies for three and four dancers, and for couples dancing *alla fila* (in a file).

Also included in the Italian treatises are instructions for *balli*, more elaborate dances with choreographies for individual couples, trios or larger ensembles. *Balli* might involve changes of tempo and metre, complex use of floor space and tricky footwork; much rehearsal would have been needed. Scenarios sometimes suggest a mimetic element; in one of the few *balli* for three couples, *Gelosia* (Jealousy), each man in turn pays more attention to the other two women than to his own partner and so provokes, one assumes, expressions of annoyance from those excluded. Although Italian *balli* are not recorded in French dance books, much interaction took place between France and Italy during the fifteenth and sixteenth centuries. One fifteenth-century Italian treatise – Giovanni Ambrosio's *De pratica seu arte tripudii* (On the Practice and Art of Dancing) – includes two *balli* from France.

The musician plays tabor and pipe, a one-man instrumental combination (the players are invariably men) often depicted accompanying genteel dance at this time (see also (18)). In the seventeenth and eighteenth centuries the tabor and pipe moved down the social scale, to be depicted chiefly in outdoor, bucolic scenes (see (32)).

In (19), also French, we move from the early to late sixteenth century; the codpiece has gone out of fashion and gentlemen wear breeches. As in the previous image there is no indication of a large-scale occasion; just four dancers and four musicians. Here the artist has captured a dance in action and demonstrates the noble ideal: feet close to the ground, graceful curves to the body and limbs and no angular or grotesque gestures. The print refutes Hogarth's assertion that an illustration 'of even the most elegant dancing ... must be always somewhat unnatural and ridiculous'.[26]

Roughly contemporary with the print is *Orchéso-graphie* (1588), already quoted and the best-known early dance treatise today. The author, Thoinot Arbeau (a pseudonym and anagram for Jehan Tabourot),

19. TWO COUPLES DANCING. (*overleaf*) n.d. The print comes with no additional information. According to Margaret McGowan the clothes are French, late sixteenth century.

was a priest in his late sixties; he lived in Langres, a provincial centre in eastern France, and the milieu he describes is less elevated than that of the couples here. A series of little woodcuts shows a man who does not wear a sword and cape as he demonstrates the steps.

Dances of the nobility are described in an Italian treatise, Fabritio Caroso's *Il Ballarino* (1581; revised in 1600 as *Nobiltà di dame*). Caroso's engravings show dancers in fine clothes, with gentlemen wearing capes and swords (see (23)). The man on the left in (19) holds the hilt of his sword, as Caroso recommends: 'When a gentleman wears a sword while dancing ... lively dances, he should hold it with his left hand, so that it will not wave around wildly.'[27] The man on the right holds his hat, which he will have removed from his head before making a *riverenza* (extended bow) at the start of the dance. As far as hat protocol is concerned, Arbeau simply advises his pupil: 'you will choose a partner who takes your fancy, and removing your hat ... with your left hand, offer her your right to lead her out to dance.'[28] Caroso, on the other hand, provides a long and detailed paragraph on the subject. He stresses that the inside of the hat should never be visible to his partner or onlookers. If the inside faces upwards, 'he reminds us of those poor cripples who beg for alms', and if it faces outwards, 'he reveals to those in front or behind him the perspiration which stains the rim of a hat'.[29] Neither Arbeau nor Caroso includes dances for two couples, but a few are to be found in another Italian treatise, Cesare Negri's *Le Gratie d'Amore* (1602).

One hundred and fifty years later a French ballroom scene depicted by court artist Charles Eisen (20) embodies notions of eighteenth-century elegance. The couple are almost certainly performing the minuet, a

dance regarded then and since as the most sublime
expression of decorum and beauty. Hogarth wrote in
The Analysis of Beauty that

> The minuet is allowed by dancing masters to be the
> perfection of all dancing. I once heard an eminent
> dancing-master say, that the minuet had been the study
> of his whole life, and that he had been indefatigable in
> the pursuit of its beauties, yet at last he could only say
> with Socrates, *he knew nothing.*[30]

Lord Chesterfield, a snob and stickler for etiquette,
advised his natural son more than once of the need to

20. SCENE IN A BALLROOM.
Charles Eisen (1720–1788),
n.d. Catalogued in an earlier
collection as *Le Menuet:
Intérieur d'un bal sous Louis
XV*, with an attribution to
Charles-Nicolas Cochin.
Eisen became a court painter
after Madame de Pompadour,
Louis XV's mistress, noticed
his talent.

45

dance well, especially the minuet. Management of the
hat remains important:

> As you will often be under the necessity of dancing a
> minuet, I would have you dance it very well. Remem-
> ber, that the graceful motion of the arms, the giving
> your hand, and the putting-on and pulling-off your hat
> genteely, are the material parts of a gentleman's danc-
> ing. But the greatest advantage of dancing well is, that it
> necessarily teaches you to present yourself, to sit, stand,
> and walk genteely; all of which are of real importance
> to a man of fashion.[31]

A gentleman wore his hat for the minuet, but
not for other dances of the period. After it had
gone out of fashion in the early nineteenth century,
dancing masters continued to recommend the minuet
as a means of achieving bearing and grace in the
ballroom: 'Minuets, Gavottes, pas Seuls, and other
movements which tend to give steadiness of carriage,
and ease in the performance of Quadrilles, and more
simple Dances, must not be neglected' is the advice
in *Lowes' Ball-Conductor and Assembly Guide*, published
in Edinburgh *c.*1820.[32] As late as the 1920s the advice
remains: 'Although it is no longer a ballroom dance
… [the minuet] is, nevertheless, considered an in-
dispensable means of training by all really educated
dancers.'[33]

Charles Eisen displayed a wide range of ages in his
drawing; two children play with a dog in the lower
left-hand corner, while in the background between the
dancers a man holding a walking stick sits next to an
elderly woman in a bonnet, shawl and muff. Another
dog frolics behind the male dancer. Dogs, symbols of
fidelity, occur in many images of social dance over
the centuries, as if to reassure the viewer that all is
as it should be between the dancers. The band in
the balcony – three fiddles, bassoon and double bass

– is an expanded version of the line-up in (5). The minuet undoubtedly dominated the eighteenth-century ballroom as a couple dance, but the Italian-born dancing master Sir John Gallini, another notorious snob (the title he used was conferred by the Pope), recommended that students should also learn dances more usually associated with the theatre, especially the *loure*, 'held by many the most pleasing of them all …; no dance affording the arms more occasion for a graceful display of them, or a more delicate regularity of the steps'.[34]

The latter part of the eighteenth century saw an increasing popularity in dances for groups rather than individual couples. *The Windsor Ball* (21) shows dancers performing what is most probably an allemande, highly fashionable at the time (the term 'allemande'

21. THE WINDSOR BALL. The date 1777, handwritten on the back of the print, is probably correct. Georgiana, Duchess of Devonshire, had recently made the absurdly high hairstyle fashionable; Lady Barrymore died in 1780 at the age of 31.

THE WINDSOR BALL.

Lady Barrymore. *Dutchess of Devonshire.* *Dutchess of Glocester.*

has, over the centuries, been applied to a number
of unrelated dances thought to have originated in
Germany). Although prominence is given to three
couples, a fourth couple, almost hidden behind the
Duchess of Devonshire and her partner, make up the
square formation of the dance. Characteristic too are
the high arm movements that result from the couples
revolving while holding both hands and bringing their
arms over each other's heads. The holding position
marks a transition between the side-by-side position
of most earlier couple dances and the front-to-front
hold of the waltz in the nineteenth century. The only
caveat in identifying the dance as an allemande is
that elements of it were incorporated into another
dance in square formation, the cotillon.

The title *Minuet Quadrille* in (22) – an oxymoron
that mixes dances from different eras – reflects
nineteenth-century nostalgia for the decorous minuet.
Queen Victoria's love of costume balls encouraged the
sentiment; she danced a minuet with Prince Albert at
a Buckingham Palace *bal costumé* in 1845. The French
conductor and composer of dances Louis Antoine
Jullien (1812–60) came to London in 1840, where he
mounted grandiose concerts involving huge orchestral
forces. His ambitious schemes led to insolvency on
several occasions and eventually to insanity. An
avowed musical popularizer, Jullien composed quadrilles based on operatic and other existing tunes;
hence the use of 'ancient melodies' in his 'Minuet
Quadrille'. His trademark piece was the 'Monster
Quadrille'. Jullien also included more serious music
in his programmes; for Beethoven he conducted 'with
a jewelled baton, and in a pair of clean kid gloves,
handed him at the moment on a silver salver'.[35] The
dedicatee of Jullien's dance, the Countess of Jersey,

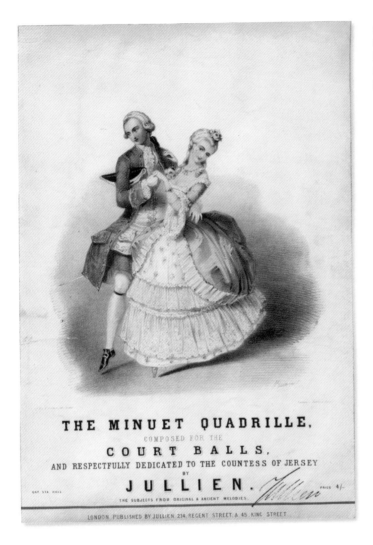

22. THE MINUET QUADRILLE.
Sheet music cover, n.d.
Published by Jullien; he had
shops at the addresses given
between 1845 and 1848.

was among those who had made the Parisian quadrille fashionable in Britain by introducing it at the
exclusive London dance venue Almack's in 1815. She
had travelled to Paris after Napoleon's banishment to
Elba in 1814, along with many other members of the
British gentry and aristocracy. As a dance for groups
of couples the quadrille supplanted the country dance
and remained popular until the early years of the
twentieth century. It had developed originally from

the cotillon, itself an offshoot of the *branle*, a French
dance of rustic origins.

Queen Victoria's love of dances from the past
coincided with growing research into dance history.
Nineteenth-century publications include Élise Voïart's
Essai sur la danse, antique et moderne (Paris, 1823), the
American dancing teacher Edward Ferrero's *The Art
of Dancing, Historically Illustrated* (New York, 1859) and
Lilly Grove's *Dancing* (London, 1895), mentioned in the
previous chapter. The two strands of historical explo-
ration, practical and theoretical, have intertwined to
produce re-creations that aim at authenticity, though
interpretation of the patchy evidence – iconographic,
textual and musical – has produced widely differing
results over the years.

FOUR

Illustrations for instruction

Dancing masters, as upholders of decorum in the
ballroom, have been cited frequently in the previous
chapter. Here we see images that relate to their work.
Dance instruction books constitute a prime source
of information for historians and re-creators of early
dance, yet the illustrations they contain often fail
to convey a sense of movement; their purpose is to
demonstrate ideal positions for particular moments
in the dance, as described in the accompanying
text. François de Lauze, author of *Apologie de la danse*
(1623), justified the lack of illustrations in his treatise
by suggesting that 'those who believe that numerous
illustrations are necessary to teach dance well from a
book' have 'more faith in the mute strokes of a dead
painting than in the energy of living eloquence'.[36]

Illustrations apart, treatises may give a distorted
view of the social dance scene generally, even within
their narrow class focus; to attract custom, dancing
masters had to strike a balance between preserving
tradition and accommodating the desire of their
young pupils for new, more exciting dances from elsewhere. All the dance types associated with the illustrations below are thought to have had rustic, provincial,
foreign or exotic backgrounds before being gentrified
by dancing masters in centres of European culture.
The *balletto* about to start in (23) might open with a
stately pavan, originally from Padua, and conclude

with a lively *canario*, believed to be from the Canaries; the very name 'country dance' (24) bespeaks rural associations; the minuet (25) developed from a rustic *branle* in the Poitou region of France, the mazurka (26) was a traditional dance from Mazovia in Poland, while the waltz mentioned in the subtitle came from the Austrian hinterland; white Americans and Britons took up jive (27) in the 1930s and 1940s as a development of the Afro-American jitterbug, while the *plena* (28) was a Puerto Rican street dance. Historians may contend these theories of origin, but their existence shows how dance teachers and pupils have enjoyed the idea of a less respectable past for their decorous

23. FROM FABRITIO CAROSO'S
IL BALLARINO. Print by
Giacomo Francho, 1581.

creations. It should be stressed that influence between classes did not flow in one direction; aspects of genteel dances and conduct naturally descended the social hierarchy too. See, for example, the description of a sixteenth-century French village festival in Chapter 6 (p. 85) and the background to the cakewalk as related in Chapter 7 (p. 103).

Although dancing masters promoted correct behaviour, they did not belong to the social rank that practised it and were liable for mockery as imitators rather than genuine practitioners of social graces. The richly dressed performers depicted in Caroso's *Il Ballarino* and *Nobiltà di dame* help to aggrandize the status of the work, which was dedicated by Caroso to his patrons, the Duke and Duchess of Parma and Piacenza. But the illustrations are scarcely necessary for teaching the dances; they merely demonstrate the opening positions and sometimes duplicate the textual descriptions. The couple in (23) illustrate the starting position for several *balletti*; in all the couple perform a *riverenza* to the first section of the music.

Four women and four men line up opposite each other for a longways country dance on the title page of *The Dancing Master* (24), the first book of dance instructions to be published in England. A hugely popular publication, it went through eighteen editions between 1651 and the late 1720s. Originally published by John Playford as *The English Dancing Master*, the books give tunes and dance instructions for country dances. The title page shown originated with the 7th edition of 1686 and the clothes must have looked very old-fashioned by 1719, the date of the edition here. With left feet forward, the dancers take the first step; typically, in the opening section of a tune, they move towards each other and back with three steps

THE DANCING SCHOOLE.

24. THE DANCING SCHOOLE.
1719. Title page for *The Dancing Master*, vol. 2. The illustration was first used in the edition of 1686, the last to be published by John Playford (1623–86), who revived English music publishing after the Civil War. Following Playford's death, publication of *The Dancing Master* passed to his son Henry (1657–*c*.1706), and after the latter's death to John Young (*fl. c.*1698–1732).

and a close (a 'double') each way, before weaving more elaborate choreographic patterns as the melody develops. The double had been a basic step unit of Renaissance dance, first described in the earliest treatises of fifteenth-century Italy and France. The illustration is titled *The Dancing Schoole*, but Cupid stands between the women and men as a hint at the true purpose behind the formalities of the lesson. He plays the fiddle with the bow used to shoot his arrows; it is more arched than the bows of the two real fiddlers either side of the dancers. The fiddlers may also be the dance teachers, one each for women and men. Dancing masters were musicians too, and played the tunes as they taught the dances.

Samuel Pepys mentioned country dances in his account of a ball at Charles II's court on New Year's Eve in 1662. First, a group of high nobility danced a *branle* together – Charles had brought back French customs from his exile during the Interregnum – after which

> the King led a lady a single Coranto; and then the rest of the lords, one after another, other ladies. Very noble it was, and a great pleasure to see. Then to Country dances, the King leading the first which he called for; which was – says he, 'Cuckolds all a-row', the old dance of England.[37]

The coranto or courant prevailed as a couple dance at balls until the last part of the seventeenth century, when it was superseded by the minuet. Country dances spanned the seventeenth and eighteenth centuries and, as Pepys indicates, would conclude a ball. Books of country dances continued to be published annually throughout the eighteenth century after *The Dancing Master* ceased publication.

The advent of Beauchamps-Feuillet dance notation in 1700 has greatly aided understanding and re-creation of eighteenth-century minuets. The notation had been developed with encouragement from Louis XIV to record the increasingly complex choreographies of social and stage dance at court; diagrams ingeniously codify steps and body movements while showing the route across the floor. In 1735 the English dancing master Kellom Tomlinson enhanced the system by including figures of dancers at various points in the dance (25); the engravings, made from Tomlinson's own designs, are among the few instructional illustrations that convey a sense of movement.

A full explanation of Beauchamps-Feuillet notation needs a book to itself, so only a brief introduction can be given here. The line that comes away from the man's left foot and curves around the bottom of the page indicates the course he takes, continued from

25. THE REGULAR ORDER OF
THE MINUET CONTINUED.
From Kellom Tomlinson's
The Art of Dancing, 1735.
Designed by Kellom
Tomlinson (*c.* 1693–*c.* 1754),
engraved by Gerard
Vandergucht (1696–1776).

the previous plate. The woman takes a symmetrical
path to the opposite side of the floor and together
the couple produce an *S* floor pattern characteristic
of the minuet. Here, the two are about to pass each
other, the closest moment in this most decorous of
dances. Either side of each route line, shorter lines

with tadpole-like heads represent the movements of
the feet (the 'heads' are the heels at the start of the
step). Intersections of the route line correspond with
bar lines in the music at the top of the page. Further
signs indicate, for example, rises and falls (*pliés*), as
well as turns of the body. Although the couples in (20)
and (25) appear similarly positioned, those in (20) are
probably further apart and at an earlier stage in the
progression of the *S* floor pattern. Steps were small
and the space taken by the dance more confined than
one might imagine.

The arrival in the ballroom of the waltz around
1800 challenged the dancing masters' command of
decorum. The face-to-face holding position, although
not adopted universally at first, shocked many, as did
the rapid turning, which made the couple dizzy and
therefore, it was thought, led to the woman losing
her self-control. Instead of being danced by one
couple at a time or in organized groups, waltzes were
performed by many couples simultaneously without
spatial interrelation. The use of floor space no longer
made a major contribution to the aesthetic apprecia-
tion of social dance and, since individual couples did
not have to display their skills to the entire company,
the ability to dance well ceased to be quite such a
social necessity.

One dancing master, Thomas Wilson, attempted
to bring the waltz under his control. In *A Description of the Correct Method of Waltzing* (1816), Wilson
strongly refuted the idea of the waltz 'as an *enemy*
to true *morals*'; instead it 'is generally admitted to
be a promoter of vigorous health, and productive
of an hilarity of spirits'. In England moreover it 'is
totally destitute of the attitudes and movements used
in warmer and lighter climates'.[38] The waltz did of

57

26. PARODI MAZURKA (OR
THE SEARING WALTZ).
Lithograph by Sarony &
Major, 1851. Music publisher
William Hall had a shop
on Broadway, New York.
The firm's name appears on
pianos, flutes and guitars
from the mid-nineteenth
century. The dedicatee,
Teresa Parodi, played leading
roles as an opera singer in
New York and on tour in the
mid-nineteenth century.

course achieve respectability, as the American couple
holding a position in the *Parodi Mazurka (or the Searing
Waltz)* demonstrate (26); the gentleman is presumably
dance teacher J.H. Searing himself. The music has
the character of a mazurka rather than a waltz, with
dotted rhythms to the melody and accents on the
third beats of most bars, yet above the score reads
'This music can be used for all the new waltzes taught
by J.M. Searing.' Hybrid dances such as the mazurka-
waltz were common at the time.

A century later, teachers faced a new challenge
to their authority from the extemporized jitterbug

and other dances of Afro-American origin associated with jazz and swing. Victor Silvester, who dominated British ballroom dance in the mid-twentieth century with his Ballroom Orchestra, 'Strict Tempo' recordings and best-selling treatise *Modern Ballroom Dancing* (1927), gave a first-hand account of the jitterbug craze and how he transformed this demotic dance for the ballroom, changing its name in the process. Silvester first became aware of the threat from jitterbug when, in 1940, his Ballroom Orchestra made a guest appearance at the Paramount dancehall in London:

> although I noticed a tendency for some of the patrons to 'truck' [a shuffling movement from Afro-American dance] to some of my band's quicksteps, they seemed to content themselves with the more or less orthodox standard dances.
>
> However ... when the resident band came on, they played jazz and the majority of the dancers started to jitterbug like mad. Some of the couples were truly spectacular and performed marvellous acrobatics, greatly to the delight of the other patrons.... For myself I watched with an interest that almost amounted to fascination.... However, it was an unusual sort of fascination. I can't say that I liked the exhibitions on the dance floor. They were too much like cabaret and quite foreign to the orthodox dances we know.... I remember thinking at the time that if jitterbug was to last, then some form of control in the dancehalls would be necessary.[39]

Silvester went on to describe how some dancehalls banned jitterbug while others 'realised that youth must have its swing and gave them every encouragement'. He concluded that jitterbug is

> a vital force providing it is modified. All lifts, throws and other exaggerated movements should be entirely eliminated. These movements are acrobatics, which is not dancing, and quite unsuitable for the ballroom. If ever this form of dancing is to develop, the standardisation of a few basic steps is essential.[40]

27. *THIS IS JIVE*. Cover
of booklet by band leader
and dance teacher Victor
Silvester (1900–1978), 1944.

After listening to diverse opinions from dancers at his weekly BBC Dancing Club broadcasts, Silvester realized that 'a modified jitterbug in one form or another was definitely wanted'. But what to call the dance? Jitterbug was in his view 'a ridiculous word'. He decided 'there was only one possible name and that was JIVE – for after all Jitterbug came to Britain from the States and the name Jive was already used extensively in that country'.[41]

The quotations come from Silvester's booklet *This is Jive* (27), published in 1944 under wartime conditions on flimsy paper (with photographs too poorly reproduced for inclusion here unfortunately). One shows a young man throwing a girl in the air; she is upside down, her underwear exposed, and illustrates Silvester's demand for the elimination of 'all lifts, throws and other exaggerated movements'. As a contrast, Silvester himself stands in white tie and tails, baton raised like a classical conductor, with the caption 'AND NOW – LET's JIVE'.[42] Victor Silvester may be viewed as the last of the musician dancing masters who had controlled ballroom decorum and etiquette for the previous five hundred years.

Jitterbug, jive and then rock'n'roll changed the face-to-face hold established by the waltz; dance partners now often danced separately. An image of couples crowding the floor and mostly dancing face-to-face (28) appears at first glance as a throwback to the waltz era. However, in the background an eleven-piece band wearing sombreros lends a Latin American flavour to the occasion, and the photo actually records a convention of New York dance teachers in 1960 performing a ballroom transformation of the *plena*, a Puerto Rican traditional dance (though the sombrero is Mexican).

Victor Silvester wrote of the risks that the ballroom dancing profession faced when introducing new material of popular origin:

> The dancing world is one peculiarly afflicted with passing fads and fancies … The difficulty of the teachers is to judge the taste of the public exactly … they have to decide whether the new feature can be put on a 'teachable' basis and whether the version they lay down will be acceptable to the dancing public in general.[43]

Unlike the tango, samba, rumba and other Latin American dances, the *plena* failed to endure in the ballroom. The teachers appear to have taken the dance a long way from its Puerto Rican street roots, if current examples of the native *plena* on YouTube are anything to go by.

28. 'DANCE MASTERS OF AMERICA (NEW YORK CITY CHAPTER) PRESENT THE PLENA, POPULAR DANCE OF PUERTO RICO, AT HOTEL EDISON ON APRIL 24TH', *c.* 1960. (The entire title handwritten on the back of the photograph; also, in a different hand: 'PLENA used Sept 60.') The *plena* was a street song before it became a dance; subject matter, as in British broadside ballads of earlier centuries, included news, local scandal, humour and love.

FIVE

Dance and desire

Passionate embraces on the dance floor clearly flout decorum, yet Renaissance treatises vary greatly in their stance towards the expression of desire; professional dancing masters paid less attention to the matter than amateur writers on dance. Domenico da Piacenza, author of the earliest surviving treatise and a professional, ignored the subject; his follower Guglielmo Ebreo made a brief allusion only, as he condemned *mechanici plebei* (the lower classes) who 'in the guise of honour ... slyly use dancing to satisfy their lust.'[44] Antonio Cornazano, also indebted to Domenico, wrote on many subjects and was not a dance professional; he recalled youthful ardour in the dedicatory preface to his *Libro dell'arte danzare* (*Book on the Art of Dancing*, *c.* 1465): 'I believed the touch of a pale hand to be total happiness and that a woman's humble and innocent glance was the cure of my misfortune. My blood was boiling in my early youth. But now I would consider shameful what I once held to be virtuous'.[45]

Antonius Arena, a soldier who went on to study law, had no such shame. Writing for his 'student companions' in the early sixteenth century, he proclaimed sexual fulfilment as the principal reason for learning to dance well: 'So then, you who desire to caress the girls and kiss them long and sweetly, must learn the correct way to dance: a thousand joys flow from the dance.'[46] Sixty years later Thoinot Arbeau,

pseudonymous author of *Orchésographie*, acknowledged
his debt to Arena, but as a retired priest toned down
the latter's ribaldry. He saw dance as a route to marriage: 'It is only natural that male and female should
seek each other … and, if you desire to marry, you
should know that a mistress is won by the pleasant
disposition and grace with which one is observed to
dance.' The passage continues: 'Dances are performed
to discover if lovers are healthy and sound of limb;
at the end men are allowed to kiss their partners;
they may touch and savour each other, to see if they
have bad breath, or body odour like a shoulder of
mutton.'[47] François de Lauze, a professional dancing
master working in England, mentioned the question
of physical attraction in a section of *Apologie de la
danse* (1623) addressed to women dancers, where he
pondered 'if the perfections of a beautiful face …
are ennobled with the graces of dance, there will be
eyes chaste enough to withstand the radiance of such
attractions without alarm'. But he advised women that
'you take offence wrongly at an innocent intention,
and it is only circumstances of time and place which
might make your behaviour culpable.'[48] Commentary
on desire comes mostly from a male perspective.

From the same period as the early Italian treatises
a French *bas de page* (29) shows three men, a Fool and
a young woman performing an apparently choreo-
graphed expression of desire in the *moresca* tradition
(see pp. 25–8 and (11)), to the music of tabor and
pipe. The men wear fashionable short doublet skirts
that enable virtuosic display, whereas the woman's
long dress and train restrict movement; her graceful
swaying contrasts with the men's angular posturing
as they vie for her attention. The dance takes place
outside, enabling the artist to integrate his performers

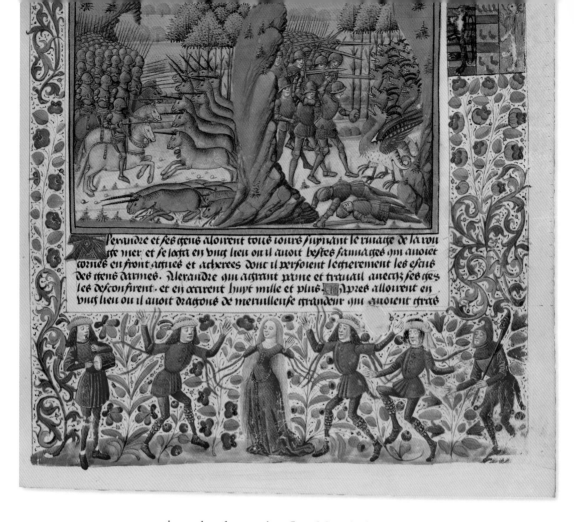

Pernudre et ses gens alloient tous tours supnant le rinage de la rou isse mer: et se losst en vng lieu ou il auoit bestes sauuages qui auoient cornes en front assies et acherees dont il persoient lestierement les esans des gens darmes. Alexandre qui achtant printe et tranail anectis ses ges les desconsirent: et en occirent buyt mille et plus. Apres alloient en vng lieu ou il auoit dragons de menulleuse grandeur qui auoient grans

into the decorative floral bordering characteristic of manuscript illumination at the time. The Fool looks older than the three men and gestures less demonstratively, yet, as we have seen, traditionally it is he who will win the woman.

Livelier Renaissance dances allowed a man to display skilled footwork, with feet taking off from the ground, but the fine line between decorum and exhibitionism shifted according to the context of performance. The Italian courtier Baldesar Castiglione, in his influential *Il libro del cortegiano* (1528, translated as *The Book of the Courtier*, 1561), made a distinction between the way a gentleman should dance before many or before few and allowed that there was a time and place to perform a *moresca*:

29. A DANCE WITH *MORESCA* CHARACTERISTICS. France, mid-fifteenth century. *Bas de page* illumination from the *Miroir du Monde*, a universal history from the Creation to the birth of Christ. Text in French. Note the wearing of bells, as in (11). A panel in the centre of the page relates to the text and shows soldiers battling with mythical beasts: unicorns on one side, and hybrids with horns and wings on the other.

if he danceth in the presence of many, and in a place
full of people, he must (in my mind) keep a certain
dignity, tempered notwithstanding with a handsome and
sightly sweetness of gestures. And for all he feeleth himself very nimble ... let him not enter into that swiftness
of feet and doubled footings, that ... were unseemly for
a gentleman: although privately in a chamber together
as we be now, I will not say but he may do both that,
and also dance the Morisco.[49]

Castiglione had warned earlier that no gentleman
would 'go about the streets dancing the morisco,
though he could do it never so well ... unless he were
clean out of his wits'.[50]

The theme of male competition for a woman occurs
in an Italian *ballo* described by Domenico, Ebreo and
Cornazano: '*Mercanzia* (Merchandise) is a *ballo* ap-
propriately named: a single woman dances with three
men, and weighs them up as if she is the merchant of
love'.[51] *Mercanzia* would have been performed inside,
with the dancers expected to display Castiglione's
'sweetness of gestures', not the antics of a *moresca*.
The Italian treatises name among the qualities of
dancing *maniera* (manner), which 'lies in the grace of
the movements you make, balancing and undulating
with the body according to the foot that moves'; *aere*
(spirit), 'an especial grace which you must have above
all others and which will make you pleasing to the
eyes of those are watching';[52] *diversita di cose* (variety);
and *compartimento di terreno* (use of space), described on
p. 39.

The expression of these qualities left no room for
the 'kissing and bussing', 'smooching and slabbering of
one another', 'filthie groping and uncleane handling'
that the puritanical writer Philip Stubbes[53] saw in
dances of his time, but a genteel couple might perhaps
demonstrate the kind of flirtation insinuated in (30).

Here desire is mutually expressed, though in different ways; the man shows off to the woman, while she casts him a sideways, flirtatious look. One cannot be certain what kind of dance they are performing, but a galliard fits the image. In this exhibitionistic six-in-a-bar dance, the man made small leaps on the first three beats and a bigger leap on the fourth beat, landing on the sixth. Sir Toby Belch, in Shakespeare's *Twelfth Night* (1.iii), encourages the foolish Sir Andrew Aguecheek to boast of his dancing prowess: 'What is thy excellence in a galliard, knight?' Sir Andrew replies 'Faith, I can cut a caper.' In 'cutting capers' the man, during the bigger leap, executed a rapid scissoring of the legs like an *entrechat* in ballet. Meanwhile the woman, restricted again by her dress, took small, demure steps opposite.

Behind the dancers two youths act as torchbearers, illuminating the young women playing harpsichord and lute, and a couple embracing on the adjacent bed. It seems unlikely that the two women form a unified dance band with the tambourine player on the right. The lutenist gazes intimately at the harpsichordist and sits close to her on the same bench, but the tambourine player stands apart, looking away from the pair. In classical imagery, tambourines are often held by Bacchantes, the wild female disciples of Bacchus; the player here may symbolize revelry and licentiousness. The harpsichord seldom appears as an instrument accompanying dance. Its presence reflects the intimate nature of the occasion and the amateur status of the female players; harpsichord and lute were among the few instruments deemed suitable for a genteel woman. The censorious text below the print translates: 'Where there is no light, dense darkness is certain to be present. Following the lust of one's flesh, he doubtless

4

neglects God's teachings: therefore he is deprived
of light and sacred oil.' Text and image encourage
censure and prurience simultaneously, just as salacious
news stories do today.

Puritanical condemnation of dance was much in
evidence at the time. Within six years, between 1577
and 1583, four works published in England railed

30. COUPLE DANCING.
Print, n.d., by Crispin de
Pas (1564–1637), designed by
Flemish artist Martin de Vos
(c. 1532–1603).

against dance: John Northbrooke's *A Treatise wherein Dicing, Dancing, Vaine Playes or Enterludes … Are Reproved* (1577), Stephen Gosson's *A Short Apologie of the Schoole of Abuse* (1579), Christopher Fetherstone's *A Dialogue against Light, Lewd, and Lascivious Dancing* (1582), and Philip Stubbes's *Anatomy of Abuses* (1583), quoted above. According to Northbrooke 'Dancing is the vilest vice of all … They dance with discordant gestures … monstrous thumping of the feet … maidens and matrons are groped and handled with unchaste hands, and kissed, and dishonestly embraced, and the things which nature hath hidden and modesty covered, are then often, by means of lasciviousness, made naked'.[54]

31. THE MISLETOE [*sic*] OR CHRISTMAS GAMBOLS. Mezzotint, n.d., designed by Edward Penny (1714–1791). The quotation beneath the title comes not from Milton as indicated, but from 'Autumn' in *The Seasons* (1730) by the Scottish poet James Thomson: 'while romp-loving miss / Is haul'd about, in gallantry robust'.

The MISLETOE or CHRISTMAS GAMBOLS.
*Whilst Romp loving Miss is hauld about
With gallantry robust*
Vide Milton.

Images (31) and (32) show changing attitudes to the
representation of plebeian dancers, so often stereotyped
as clumsy in genre prints and paintings over previous
centuries (see the next chapter). Edward Penny's *The
Misletoe or Christmas Gambols* (31) gives a sentimental
view of life below stairs, as dancers enjoy behaviour
that would not be countenanced in the ballroom; three
couples cavort flirtatiously beneath the mistletoe, while
a fourth couple kiss and embrace in the background.
Generally, graceful curves replace the angular postures
of de Bry's rustic dancers. Penny remains largely
forgotten today, but had a distinguished career; he was
appointed the first Professor of Painting at London's
Royal Academy and prints based on his paintings of
moral subjects sold in large numbers.

Isaac Cruikshank – father of the better-known
George (see (44)) – produced caricatures from all

32. DANCE ON A GRAVESEND
BOAT. Isaac Cruikshank
(*c.* 1756–1811), n.d. Amy Miller,
Curator of Decorative Arts
and Material Culture at the
national Maritime Museum,
London, writes 'Although
sailors did not have regulated
dress until 1857, they did wear
a type of "uniform" clothing
that was easily identifiable,
such as the short blue jacket
and trousers. They would
also have held with fashion,
which can be seen with the
style of the waistcoat. Due to
the practice of selling clothes
at the mast, sailors were able
to pick up very nice second
hand clothes. The black hat
was often straw or felt that
had been covered with a
waterproofed oilcloth. Often,
they would paint their ship's
name on it.'

sections of society, yet in *Dance on a Gravesend Boat* (32) he sympathetically portrays a naval rating and young woman dancing to the music of a fiddler and taborer. Neither dancer is upper class, but their bodies and limbs show graceful curves, without angularity. Isaac Cruikshank's contemporary Thomas Rowlandson often focused on relations between the sexes (his prolific output includes a number of sexually explicit prints). The public masquerade (33), with its reputation for depravity, made a natural target for the artist. Initiated in London by the theatre manager John Jacob Heidegger a hundred years before *Masquerading*, masquerades quickly achieved notoriety, not only for sexual promiscuity, but because social classes intermingled freely, their status disguised by masks and costumes. Moral censure only succeeded in attracting more people to the events and made Heidegger a great deal of money. Hogarth had satirized Heidegger's masquerades in his early prints *Masquerades and Operas* and *Masquerade Ticket*.

On the far right stands an academic, whose hand appears slyly from his gown to tickle the bottom of a woman in breeches (cross-dressing roles abounded in the theatre). The central, partially hidden Punch-like figure dances as he strums on a cittern or English guitar. A woman carries a tome titled *Magi* in her left hand and a long thin wand in her right, while a man in Eastern garb and sandals gazes at her. The magi were followers of the ancient Persian astrologer and sorcerer Zoroaster; the word 'magic' derives from *magi*. The sign 'Horns to sell' alludes to the horn as a symbol of cuckoldry; cuckold's horns sprout from a head just below. The women are young and attractive, the men old and ugly.

33. MASQUERADING. Thomas Rowlandson (1756–1827), 1811.

HORNS
TO SELL

MAGI

MASQUERADING.

DUBLIN.
HENRY BUSSELL.
PRICE 2/6

34. THE SPIRIT OF THE BALL,
n.d. Lithograph by Forster
of Dublin; artist unknown.
Detail from sheet music
cover for a galop by Lord
Otho Augustus FitzGerald
(1827–1882). Published by
Henry Bussell, who operated
under that name, at the
address given on the cover,
from c. 1857 to 1874.

Half a century later sensibilities had changed;
the association of grotesque ugliness with lechery is
implied rather than stated in (34), a detail from a
mid-Victorian sheet music cover for a galop, *The Spirit
of the Ball*; the galop had entered the ballroom around
1830 as the 'galopade'. Again, male ugliness contrasts
with female beauty. The odd creatures, many with
animal heads, sprout tails and are strangely attired;
the figure on the right appears be naked apart from
a short skirt. Behind, an orchestra includes further
animal grotesques as well as Chinese figures. The
simple, energetic galop had no reputation for sensuality or immorality; it was considered good clean fun
and often concluded a ball.

Dances that have incurred moral censure over the
centuries on account of their perceived sensuality
include the volta, sarabande, waltz and tango. In the
volta, a development of the galliard in the second half
of the sixteenth century, the woman took an active
role; it was she and not the man who made the big

jump during the fourth and fifth beats of the bar.
The man encouraged her upwards through nudging
her from behind with his left thigh, while gripping
the busk of her corsetry at the front with his right
hand and swinging her round clockwise as he turned
on the spot. The volta broke all rules of decorum;
Arbeau asked if 'both honour and health are not
threatened'[55] in performing the dance. The sarabande,
banned in Spain for its obscenity in 1583, transformed
itself over the next century from a fast dance into the
slowest movement of the baroque suite and the slowest
stage dance; in 1708 Kellom Tomlinson composed a
sarabande choreography in Feuillet notation for a solo
male, laden with complex steps and marked in his
manuscript 'Very slow'.[56] (It should be mentioned that
other long-lived dances changed as the years passed,
with regional variations developing too. The minuet
and waltz, for example, altered considerably over their
extended life spans.)

While waltz and sarabande became thoroughly respectable over time, the tango (35) has always retained
its historical reputation as a sensual dance, despite
several transformations in the ballroom over the past
century. Stories of its disreputable and exotic origins
abound: 'In the drinking shops and bordellos [of
Buenos Aires] … seamen and gauchos competed for
the favours of the half-Indian habituées. … Becoming
habituated with the habanera rhythm … they immediately adopted it and from it created their insidious
tango.'[57] The dance slowly achieved respectability in
Paris during the first decade of the twentieth century
and in London before the outbreak of World War I.
A short-lived craze for the dance ensued, which faded
with the war. Interest revived somewhat after the war
with an altered version of the dance (the period of

the so-called *Tango authentique* illustrated here), but did not really pick up again until about 1930; considerable variations in style then developed. Performers do not necessarily share the viewers' perception of tango, since their overriding priority is to concentrate on the movement style and complex steps that convey the sensuality of the dance. More than any other twentieth-century social dance, tango has a theatrical quality, aimed at the onlooker.

Images from this chapter show that in illustrating dance, as in actual performance, desire is usually expressed by implication rather than overt demonstration. For fulfilment, dancing has to stop, as it has for the couple on the bed in (30) and for the couple kissing in the background of (31).

35. BRAZILIAN BEAUTIES: TANGO AUTHENTIQUE, n.d. M. Kay Jerome had several dances published in the late 1910s. American music publishers Waterson, [Irving] Berlin and Snyder dominated Tin Pan Alley for much of the 1910s and 1920s. The tango originated in Argentina, not Brazil.

SIX

Rustic revels

From tango and other ballroom dances with less than respectable origins the spotlight now shifts to dancing untouched by gentrification, as portrayed during the sixteenth and seventeenth centuries in Germany and the Low Countries. The images provide a broader social and illustrative context to Théodore de Bry's rustic dancers in (3).

The grotesque couple in (36) would have been familiar to many in Germany from the tale *Solomon and Marcolf*, which recounts a battle of wits between King Solomon and the unsavoury but clever peasant Marcolf. The king, hearing of Marcolf's reputation, commands his presence. He challenges Marcolf: 'If you can reply to my utterances in their entirety, I will enrich you with great riches and you will be most renowned in my realm.' Marcolf replies: 'The priest promises a well-being over which he has no power'.[58] Solomon proceeds with a string of lofty maxims, which Marcolf subverts with impudent, scatological and sexually obscene retorts. Around fifty editions of the book were published between the late fifteenth and early seventeenth centuries.

Daniel Hopfer may have taken the idea of representing Marcolf and Politana as a dancing couple from Dürer's *Peasant Couple Dancing* (1514), mentioned in Chapter 1. Hopfer makes Marcolf and his wife

BOLIKANA · D ⚜ H · MARKOLFVS

36. BOLIKANA AND
MARCOLFUS (Politana and
Marcolf). Daniel Hopfer
(c. 1470–1536), n.d. A German
designer and printmaker,
Hopfer pioneered etching
techniques that were
used by his more famous
contemporary Albrecht
Dürer.

much uglier than Dürer's couple, to match the tone of
the textual description:

Marcolf was short and squat. He had a great big head;
a very broad, red, and wrinkled forehead; ears that
were hairy and hung all the way down to the middle of
his jaws; fat and bleary eyes; a lower lip like a horse's; a
dirty beard that reeked like a goat's; stubby hands; short
and squat fingers; round feet; a thick and bulging nose;

76

large and flat lips; a face like a donkey's; hair thick like the spines of hedgehogs ... His wife too was little and very squat with thick breasts. She had spiky hair; eyebrows that bristled like a pig's back, a beard like a goat; ears like a donkey's; bleary eyes; a snake-like face.[59]

The nest and roosting bird in Marcolf's hair (the jay is sometimes called a 'Marcolf' in Germany), the bells round his neck and the chatelaine dangling from Politana's waist are not mentioned in the text. The chatelaine features in Dürer's image, as it does in many later prints of peasant dancers (see (39) and (40)). Like Dürer's couple, Marcolf and Politana have the angular knees so often associated with uncouth dancing; Politana holds her skirt to reveal a bare knee.

Dancing featured prominently at rural festivals in Germany and the Low Countries, including the annual country fair or 'kermis', which celebrated the founding or saint's day of a local church and lasted several days. Kermis images that I have seen invariably include dancing; in (37) three couples perform together as they would in an English country dance or French *branle*. Each man has his right foot on the ground and left leg raised, and each couple joins hands with arms raised; high arm movements eventually entered genteel dance in the late-eighteenth-century allemande (see (21)). As in many similar scenes, a bagpiper accompanies.

Other components of kermis images include drinking and eating at a table outside a tavern; vomiting (a woman lower right, and a man above her, leaning against a building on the right); games (a forerunner of croquet takes places behind the building); violence (a fight, to the right of the table); and a church in the background to remind us that the occasion for

37. KERMIS SCENE. (*overleaf*) Designed by Pieter van der Borcht (1545–1608), n.d. Dürer's pupil Sebald Beham (1500–1550) originated the kermis or country fair as a subject for prints; it remained popular with German, Flemish and Dutch artists, including the Flemish designer Pieter van der Borcht in the later sixteenth century. At the time of Beham's prints Lutheran disapproval and ordinances threatened the kermis.

77

licentious behaviour is a religious festival. Further
details in van der Borcht's print include a toy vendor,
far lower left, selling windmills, toy drums and hobby
horses; the woman buying a toy windmill has her
purse cut by a man stooping behind her. A hurdy-
gurdy player with dog importunes the banqueters
at the table. To the left of the croquet-type game a
drummer plays by a small group of men and women
with staves, suggesting that another dance or procession is imminent. Verses below the print describe the
activities without moral judgement.

The virtuosic egg dance (38) entertained participants and spectators alike at annual festivals, including Easter. Many different versions existed throughout
Europe, some involving several eggs and performers.
The solo dancer here performs with a single egg, to
music from a bagpiper: hopping in time, he has to roll
the egg to the ground from the top of an upturned
bowl and then attempt to place the bowl over the
egg, all within a circumscribed space. 'It's like the egg
dance' is a German saying for difficult tasks.[60] Dance
at country festivals could be highly competitive, with
prizes offered. The print incorporates further elements
found in scenes of dancing and entertainment: the
bagpiper's position under a tree; the couple in the
foreground sitting with their backs to the viewer and
arms around each other, a dog at their feet nearby
and the presence or invasive entrance of performers on mock instruments. The duo here wearing
kitchen implements play knife on gridiron, and tongs
strummed by fingers fitted with plectra. Similar
figures appear, for example, in Bruegel's *Battle between
Carnival and Lent*. Rustic scenes may include a figure
or figures from a higher social rank surveying the
activities. Here, a young couple in fine clothes watch

Mart. De Vos inuent.

Ioan. Baptista Vrints ex.

the performance; the antics of country folk provide
amusement, as they do for viewers of the print. In
the background three couples, with similar gestures
to those in (37), dance to a second bagpiper. Other
artists from the Low Countries who depicted egg
dances include Pieter Aertsen (1508–75), Pieter Bruegel
the younger (c. 1564–1636) (danced by a woman) and
Jan Steen (1625/6–79); the latter's painting shows a
spirited circle dance around the egg.

Verses below the image deride the activity; the
opening line translates: '[Only] a sick person would
laugh seeing these mad folk dance.' Texts for rustic
scenes vary in tone and attitude, ranging from a rose-
tinted approval of the peasants' Arcadian life – 'Ah,

38. THE EGG DANCE.
Designed by Marten de
Vos (1532–1603), n.d. A
leading Flemish painter after
Bruegel's death in 1569, de
Vos produced designs for
many prints, especially in the
early 1580s. See also (30).

39. A RUSTIC MARRIAGE
FEAST, n.d. Drawn for a print
inscribed with the initials
and logo of the Dutch painter
and engraver Adriaen van
der Venne (1589–1662). The
print is reversed and therefore
shows the man holding the
woman's left hand with his
right hand, as was customary
in Renaissance and baroque
dance; see for example the
couples in (5), (19), (36) and
(37).

too fortunate the peasants, if they were to know their blessings'[61] – to contempt and moral censure.

In (39) a wedding feast provides the occasion for dance. The central figure at the table wearing a crown is the bride. Either side of her an older man and woman, her parents one assumes, argue across her. A second couple sit to the right of the picture; the woman does not like what she hears from her neighbours. The backcloth hung behind the table features in other wedding scenes, including Bruegel's *Peasant Wedding Feast* and *Peasant Wedding Dance*, and David Teniers the younger's *Peasant Wedding* a century later. Bruegel shows a single crown suspended above the bride's head; Teniers, like van der Venne, has three.

The dancing couple, dressed in their best clothes, have exchanged hats; the man sitting behind them gestures to his own hat in puzzlement. The male dancer looks down gracelessly at his feet, while his partner dances confidently. To the left of the bride and her parents a man stands and raises his arms, hat in hand (see a similar figure at the table in (37)). In front of the table a young mother looks on with mild amusement while a dog licks her baby's bottom. A bagpiper accompanies, but looks away from the dancers, uninvolved; beside him a man vomits and a dog licks up the mess. The latter activity occurs in the earliest known wedding print, by the German engraver Erhard Schön a hundred years or so before (1527).

These festive scenes convey the energy and vigour of rustic dancing, qualities which are corroborated by Arena in a contemptuous description:

> When our country folk dance they throw themselves about and do not even observe the beat. They run continually ... and invent everything out of their heads.

... At the beginning of the dance they doff their caps too soon and without grace and shuffle their legs. They make the reverence so vigorously that, believe me, they turn up a spadeful of soil with their foot. They do the branles boisterously, country style, and everyone thinks himself a past master of dancing. They keep this up until the taborer is exhausted. ... Peasant folk never keep time when they are dancing, and they know very little about doubles and singles.[62]

Arena's purpose was to emphasize through contrast the structured progression of the genteel, restrained *basse danse*, the principal topic of his treatise. He concluded: 'even if they were to learn the basse dance, these rustics would not be able acquire the style'.[63] In fact, the synchronized movements in (37) would be impossible if the dancers never kept time or observed the beat; in art and literature, satirical exaggeration of rustic behaviour bolstered class prejudices. Literary historian Eric Auerbach observed that 'The comic and frivolously erotic, the satirical, realistic, and obscene' were all 'subjects ... assigned to the lower class.'[64] Auerbach was writing of the levels of discourse in literature – sublime, middling and low – that had continued into the Middle Ages and Renaissance from Roman antiquity, and his observation applies to the content and treatment of festive prints and paintings.

But a few writers in the Renaissance provided a different perspective, as Margaret McGowan has shown. Claude Gauchet, in his description of dancing at a village festival, related how the most skilful performed courtly galliards and how, as in genteel dance, too much exhibitionism encouraged mockery. Montaigne and the poet Philippe Desportes both praised the lightness and skill of young country women as they danced. According to Gauchet's account, first prize went to the person who danced *plus dispost* (most nimbly), *plus gaillard* (with most spirit) and *plus sage* (most decorously).[65] These qualities were admired in genteel dance.

Who bought prints and paintings in the Low Countries? Not just the rich, according to seventeenth-century traveller Peter Mundy in his report of life in Amsterdam:

> As for the art of painting and the affection of the people to pictures, I think none other go beyond them. ... All in general striving to adorn their houses, especially the outer or street room, with costly pieces, butchers and bakers not much inferior in their shops, which are fairly set forth, yea many times blacksmiths, cobblers, etc., will have some picture or other by their forge and in their stall. Such is the general notion, inclination and delight that these country native[s] have to paintings.[66]

The passage draws attention to tradesmen and craftsmen who lived more comfortably than the peasantry; they too played a part in festive celebrations. The use of the word 'peasant' in titles given to kermis and wedding scenes gives a misleading impression of a two-tier society.

Prints and paintings produced for public consumption presented easily recognisable caricatures of country folk entertaining themselves; the couple in (40), privately recorded in an *album amicorum* (book of friends), are portrayed more sympathetically. The illustration nevertheless incorporates traditional features of dancing peasant iconography. As in (36), the woman reveals her knees and also her petticoat. There are similarities too to the dancers in (39); each woman wears an apron and chatelaine and each man wears a codpiece, which had gone out of fashion in genteel society by the end of the sixteenth century.

The compiler of an *album amicorum* was often a young scholar or academic; images in Jan van der

Deck's album range widely in subject matter, with coats of arms (a typical inclusion), finely dressed dignitaries, a couple in masks and costumes, a woman carried in a chaise, street vendors, two women in a grand coach, a hunter with a rifle, and a woman with a basket full of game. Commentaries are written in Latin, German, Italian and French. Adriaen van der Venne, who presumably drew (39), also compiled an album of watercolours (now in the British Museum). It includes two illustrations of dancing peasant couples, one a close copy of his dancers in (39), executed with less caricature, and the other of a woman dancing with a sailor; she holds an identical pose to van der Deck's female dancer. Similar too are the folds in their skirts and aprons, and the way their chatelaines

40. DANCING COUPLE. From the *album amicorum* of Jan van der Deck, n.d. Many images on previous pages in the album are dated 1592.

87

41. LA REINE DE LA FÈVE. Jan Verbeeck (*fl. c.* 1548–60), n.d. The Flemish artist is known only from a small number of drawings. The title comes from K.T. Parker's catalogue of drawings in the Ashmolean; it does not appear on the drawing.

j. verbecc 15 . 60

W.Y.O.

swing out. The two images must surely derive from a common source or from mutual acquaintance. Apparent realism does not necessarily indicate a figure drawn from life.

Dance forms part of Christmas festivities in (41). The title *La reine de la fève* translates literally as 'The queen of the bean'; dictionaries give 'queen of Twelfth Night'. The expression derives from the custom of appointing a mock king and queen on the twelfth day of Christmas following the discovery of a bean (for the king) and pea (for the queen) in slices of a large cake, known as the *gâteau des rois* (cake of kings). The couple then oversee the Twelfth Night revels. Here, the elderly queen looks aghast at her much younger king as they perform a line dance with five others (the line curves round behind the man on the right of the picture to include two figures with their backs to us). Images of bean feasts about a century later, by Jan Steen, Gabriel Metsu and Jacob Jordaens, show an old man wearing the crown.

Explanations for other activities in the picture remain speculative. A man behind the queen seems to be arranging her unkempt hair, or maybe has just positioned her crown. In a window or balcony above the dancers a man and a woman gesticulate with crutches, while another man looks sadly on, resting his cheek on the back of his hand. Perhaps expectations of almsgiving have not been realized. As in (39) and other wedding scenes, a backcloth hangs behind a table. Two men grapple with an object on the table – one sticks his tongue out at the other – while on the far left of the picture a group of men in tall hats carrying Dutch hoes have entered the room. In front, a shawm player with plumed hat provides music; a bagpipe hangs at his waist.

The unusualness of Verbeeck's scene suggests it may have derived from an actual occasion rather than the re-assembling of familiar ingredients to create an imagined festivity. Routine copying of gestures and activities raises questions about the realism of festive scenes in general and the dancing in particular. Many of the dancers we have seen in this chapter follow rustic stereotypes. In each image one dancer or more holds the 'knees-up' position that so often signifies dance that violates decorum. Do these portrayals give an accurate impression of popular dancing over a period of more than a hundred years? Symbols often lag behind the times; for example, the warning sign in Britain for a level crossing without barriers is an obsolete steam engine. Sayings likewise may fail to reflect the present. In a largely urban society we talk about making hay while the sun shines, not looking a gift horse in the mouth, and not counting chickens before they hatch. And we still use the expression 'a knees-up'.

SEVEN

Burlesquing the bourgeois

Middle-class mishaps replace rustic clumsiness in nineteenth-century satire of social dance. The prints in (42), (43) and (44) were published by Hannah Humphrey, whose shop in St James's Street stood at the heart of London's clubland and around the corner from Almack's, the exclusive dance assembly rooms in King Street. One can imagine the gentry and nobility enjoying the humour of ballroom gaffes posted among the political satires in Humphrey's shop window, as they made their way to Almack's or a club. An illustration by Humphrey's associate James Gillray shows every pane of glass framing a print, as heavily coated gentlemen peer in.

'We must ... mind our P's and Q's at ALMACKS ... It is the rallying point of *rank*, wealth, talents, and beauty: it is, likewise, the meridian of fashion, style, elegance, and manners, from the *alpha* to the *omega*',[67] says man-about-town Tom to country squire Jerry in Pierce Egan's *Life in London* (1821). Another chronicler of early-nineteenth-century life, Captain Gronow, looked back on the year 1814 and recalled 'One can hardly conceive the importance which was attached to getting admission to Almack's, the seventh heaven of the fashionable world.' Gronow continued that the dances at Almack's then 'were Scotch reels and the old English country-dance'. He claimed that the 'mazy waltz' was introduced around that time, but 'there were comparatively few who at first ventured to whirl around the salons of Almack's'.[68] It has been stated that 'although the waltz was danced at Almack's Assembly Rooms by foreigners prior to 1812, London society resisted it until its appearance on the program of a ball given in July 1816 by the Prince Regent.'[69]

The print *Waltzer au Mouchoir* (1800) (literally, 'to waltz to a handkerchief') (42) confirms that waltzing had reached England at a less elevated level well before it was accepted at Almack's. A handkerchief

42. WALTZER AU MOUCHOIR. Attributed to James Gillray (1756–1815), 1800. Published by Hannah Humphrey (*c.* 1745–1818). Gillray lived above Humphrey's shop.

London. Publish'd Jan.' 20.' 1800. by H. Humphrey. 27. S.' James's Street.

Waltzer au Mouchoir.

waltz described in Henri Cellarius's *Drawing-Room Dances* (1847) might explain the ill-matched partnership: 'The first couple sets out. After the waltze [*sic*] or promenade, the lady makes a knot in one of the four corners of a handkerchief, which she presents to four gentlemen. He who hits upon the knot waltzes or dances with her to her place.'[70] *Waltzer au Mouchoir* shows two features of the waltz that distinguished it so markedly from the minuet: the presence of several couples dancing independently (two further couples dance in the background), and the much censured face-to-face holding position. A horn, symbol of cuckoldry, is the one instrument visible in the balcony band, upper left. In Lord Byron's satire *The Waltz* (1813), ingenuous country gentleman Horace Hornem reacts to his wife's waltzing at a fashionable London ball: 'Judge of my surprise, on arriving, to see poor dear Mrs. Hornem with her arms half round the loins of a huge hussar-looking gentleman I never set eyes on before; and his, to say truth, rather more than half round her waist, turning round and round to a d—d see-saw up-and-down sort of tune.'[71] The whirling and turning that feature in many early accounts of waltzing suggest that the term – from the German *walzen*, meaning then 'to turn' – indicated rapid rotation rather than a particular step pattern.

The handkerchief waltz injected a random element into the selection of partners; choice otherwise lay with the man. Over the centuries etiquette made it hard for a woman to refuse a request, however repellent she might find the man inviting her. In *A broad hint of not meaning to Dance* (43) (1804), the woman not only picks up her chair to evade an invitation, but also tears her gown as she moves away; the man has trodden on it. More than two hundred years earlier,

in *Orchésographie*, Arbeau's pupil Capriol had worried
that 'if the young woman refused me I should be
thoroughly shamed'.[72] His teacher reassures him that
refusal would make the woman, not him, look foolish.
Male pride must be protected.

Surprisingly, Arbeau did not mention that either
gender could request a dance in the sixteenth century.
In 'A Lady's Conduct When Inviting a Gentleman
to Dance' from *Nobiltà di dame*, Caroso stressed the
need for a woman to display discretion and modesty,
but warned that too much reticence caused confusion
when asking a man to dance: 'some ... cast their eyes
so low that the gentlemen cannot tell which one of
them has been invited, so that one rises to his feet
rather than the other. Or ... they [all] give her their
hands, with the result that she does not know which
one to take.'[73] Arena's women show no diffidence:
'Beautiful women will beg you to dance with them
and furthermore they will often require perforce that
you do so.' It was unwise to refuse: 'If you will not
dance when the damsel desires, your charming friend
will, out of courtesy, say nothing, but her vexation
will create antipathy where agreement would have
fostered love.'[74] It is not known if female invitation was
a regional practice, or when it died out, as it certainly
had by the nineteenth century. *The Ball-room Guide*
(1866) advises women that

> To accept is easy enough – 'Thank you,' is sufficient;
> to decline with delicacy, and without giving offence, is
> more difficult – "Thank you, I am engaged,' suffices
> when that expresses the fact – when it does not, and a
> lady would rather not dance with the gentleman apply-
> ing to her, she must beg to be excused, as politely as
> possible, and it is in better taste for her not to dance at
> all in that set. The slightest excuse should suffice, as it is
> ungentlemanly to force or press a lady to dance.[75]

43. A BROAD HINT OF
NOT MEANING TO DANCE.
James Gillray, 1804, after a
design by Brownlow North.
Published by Hannah
Humphrey.

~~~20~~~1804, by H Humphrey N° 27, St James's Street

uaning to Dance.

Background detail from *A broad hint of not meaning to Dance* again reveals changing practices in the early 1800s; such a confused scrum of dancers would have been unthinkable for much of the previous century (see (4), (20) and (21)).

The nineteenth century has been named 'the century of waltz',[76] but 'the century of quadrille' would be as appropriate. After its introduction to England at Almack's in 1815 the dance spread rapidly, and by 1817, the date of *Les Graces – Inconveniences in Quadrille Dancing* (44), its popularity was established. Half a century later *The Ball-room Guide* recommended that 'A ball should commence with a quadrille, followed by a waltz. Quadrilles and waltzes, including galops, indeed form the chief feature of the modern ball.'[77] A sample dance programme 'as used at Her Majesty's balls, given at Buckingham Palace' largely alternates quadrilles and waltzes; a few lancers (another quadrille) and galops provide the only variety.[78]

Group dances such as country dances and quadrilles could expose incongruities of ability and physical traits, as Hogarth had demonstrated in his country dance scene (4). Discrepancies in skill became more apparent during the nineteenth century, as the need to dance well declined in importance. During the eighteenth and early nineteenth centuries skilful ballroom dancers incorporated steps and movements from theatrical dance; the dancing masters who taught them were themselves professional dancers. When the quadrille arrived, adept performers continued for a while to display balletic steps. In 'A mishap at Almack's', Captain Gronow described how Lord Graves, 'who was extremely fat', engaged 'the beautiful Lady Harriet Butler one evening as his partner in a quadrille'. Lord Graves wanted to imitate Lady

Butler's 'graceful ease' in making *entrechats*, but fell heavily to the floor in the attempt.[79] Criticism of his behaviour almost provoked a duel. Two pictures on the wall in the background of *Inconveniences in Quadrille Dancing* contrast a pair of quasi-acrobatic ballet dancers on the left with an ungainly rustic couple on the right.

As the century progressed, elaborate steps disappeared from the quadrille. One might have expected disapproval from dancing masters, but Henri Cellarius pondered: 'The youthful dancers of the present day, who are accused so often of walking, instead of dancing, are they, then, so wrong in renouncing the *entrechats*, the *ronds de jambes*, and other complicated steps used in former days...?'[80] From the same period American dancing master Charles Durang advocated

44. LES GRACES – INCONVENIENCES IN QUADRILLE DANCING. George Cruikshank (1792–1878), 1817. Published by Hannah Humphrey. The quadrille was danced by groups of four couples to a sequence of five tunes with associated routines. Here, a pianist, presumably amateur, provides the music; her presence, rather than that of a professional dance band, suggests a small-scale, informal occasion.

Les Graces
Inconveniences in Quadrille Dancing

P. 3.

G Cruikshank fet

Pub.ª April 9.th 1817 by
H Humphrey 27 St James's St.

the quadrille because 'the stout and the slender, the light and the ponderous, may mingle in its easy and pleasant evolutions with mutual satisfaction. Even a slight mistake committed by the unskillful in this dance, will not incommode a partner, or interrupt the progress of the movement.'[81]

Printed dance programmes, mentioned above, were recommended by *The Ball-room Guide* for any private ball that was 'more than a mere "carpet-dance"'.[82] The picture on the programme in (45) demonstrates Victorian nostalgia for the eighteenth century as an era of bygone elegance; the reverse side (46) gives the sequence of dances for the evening, with space for guests to write their partners' names with the attached pencil. Note the names or initials faintly scribbled in. The mix of dances belongs to the second half of the nineteenth century, and includes several that took hold from the middle years: polka, caledonians (a quadrille), mazurka, varsoviana, schottische and circassian. The polka was the most popular. As with many ballroom dances it is supposed to have a rustic origin: 'In Eastern Bohemia Josef Neruda saw a peasant girl, Anna Chadimova, extemporise this dance, singing her own accompaniment and making up the steps as she went along.'[83] It is said that Neruda, a Czech organist and music teacher, wrote down the tune and had Anna teach the steps to students. Polkas were fashionable in Paris from about 1843; the mazurka, a Polish dance of folk origin, came into fashion shortly

after. Elements of polka and mazurka steps were com-
bined in the varsoviana, a Parisian concoction from
the 1850s. Caledonians appeared on programmes from
the 1830s. The schottische – German for 'Scottish
dance' – may actually have originated in Germany.
It spread through Europe in the 1850s. Circassia is
a region of the Caucasus with a tradition of circle
dances; the ballroom circassian started in a circle for
as many as cared to join and often ended a ball.

The programme in (46) appears varied, but in fact
quadrille (including lancers and caledonians) and
waltz dominate. Remaining dances comprise three
polkas (including a polka quadrille), two mazurkas,
one schottische and the concluding circassian.
The Ball-room Guide, after stating that
quadrilles and waltzes should form the
main feature of a ball, continues: 'a
polka, a schottische, a polka mazourka,
or even a varsoviana, may be thrown in
as an occasional relief, just as a country
dance is often tolerated as a finale; but
these dances are only tolerated.'[84] The
comment appears to underestimate the
popularity of the polka. An assembly
rooms programme for 1848 comprises five
quadrilles, four polkas and three waltzes;
half a century later, a programme for a state
ball at Buckingham Palace consists entirely
of quadrilles, waltzes and polkas in rotation,
with a galop at the end.

From the latter part of the nineteenth
century onwards British social dance responded
increasingly to American influence. The barn
dance – another name with rustic associations
– crossed the Atlantic in the late 1880s. Steps derived

46. DANCE PROGRAMME.
Reverse side, n.d.

Dances.

1. Polka ....
2. Quadrille ....
3. Valse ....
4. Lancers ....
5. Valse ....
6. Caledonians ....
7. Mazurka ....
8. Valse ....
9. Quadrille ....
10. Varsoviana ....
11. Schottische ....
12. Lancers ....
13. Valse ....
14. Polka Quadrille ....
15. Valse ....
16. Lancers ....
17. Polka ....
18. Caledonians ....
19. Valse ....
20. Mazurka ....
21. Circassian and Valse ....
M.-C.'s—G. R. Davies.   J. Simms.
A. Meynell.   S. Simpson.
W. Haithwaite, *Hon. Sec.*

47. A MIDSUMMER NIGHT.
NEW BARN DANCE. Image by
H.G. Banks, for sheet music
cover, 1891. The barn dance
had originally been associated
with the tune 'Dancing in the
Barn'. H.G. Banks made a
number of designs for sheet
music covers either side of
1900; they include music-hall
songs performed by Marie
Lloyd, Vesta Tilley and Dan
Leno.

from the scottische, and the dance 'was to be found
on every programme for a number of years, certainly right through the first decade of the twentieth
century.'[85] In (47) a thoroughly respectable gentleman
and his partner shock an onlooker as their enjoyment

of the 'new barn dance' *A Midsummer Night* leads them to execute a knees-up (though the woman is constrained by her gown). Perhaps no image in the book demonstrates more clearly how perceived rustic origins for a dance encouraged genteel dancers to push the bounds of propriety by behaving more exuberantly than usual.

At about the same time that the barn dance found its way into white American ballrooms, the cakewalk (48) gained notice as the finale of Afro-American staged shows. It had originated more informally as a send-up of white affectations: 'Us slaves watched white folks' parties, where the guests danced a minuet and then paraded in a grand march … Then we'd do it, too, *but we used to mock 'em*, every step. Sometimes the white folks noticed it, but they seemed to like it; I guess they thought we couldn't dance any better.' The quotation is attributed to a nurse, recalling her childhood in the American South during the 1840s.[86] The name 'cakewalk', recorded from 1889, comes from the prizes that were offered in dance competitions, 'first, ice cream and chocolates; later on, huge decorated cakes. At the end the winner cut the cake and shared it with the other dancers.'[87] Virtuosic performances developed that included 'prancing and high-kicking with back arched and toe pointed',[88] a description that matches the posture of the performer on the right

48. AT THE CAKE-WALK JUBILEE. Small detail from a sheet music cover published by Will Rossiter, Chicago, 1915. The full title reads '"*Some Steppers, Hot Peppers*" At the Cake-walk Jubilee, As Originally Introduced by Bob Allan and Billy Stoneham.'

49. BAD DANCING. Dan Piraro, 2003. Note that the man entering the party has a stick of dynamite, fuse lit, protruding from the back pocket of his jeans.

in (48). As part of the satire, cakewalk dancers took to wearing elegant costumes, 'the men in long-tailed coats with high collars, the women in fluffy white gowns with bouquets of flowers';[89] again the illustration replicates the description. The image forms a small detail on a sheet music cover *At the Cake-Walk Jubilee*, the main feature of which is a photograph of white performers Bob Allan and Billy Stoneham, in fanciful drag and tails respectively, apparently burlesquing an Afro-American dance that was itself a burlesque of white performance.

Finally, to bring the imagery full circle, a dance hieroglyph for the twenty-first century (49). Cartoonist Dan Piraro has altered the public sign that warns of a slippery floor to denote bad dancing instead. The posture of the off-balance figure with one knee and arms raised is mimicked by dancers enjoying the party in the background. The 'knees-up' posture occurs in more than a third of the images in this book. Absent from the chapters 'Decorous Dance' and 'Illustrations for Instruction', and present throughout 'Rustic Revels', from the Renaissance onwards it has been used to distinguish class or social rank. Although the posture may indicate a breach of decorous behaviour, it does not necessarily signify bad dancing. It may also suggest energy, exhibitionism, exuberance and enjoyment: qualities much in evidence when rock'n'roll displaced the tired routines of waltz and quickstep in the 1950s.

Notes

Full details of works cited are given in the Bibliography.
Translations are by the author, unless stated otherwise.

1. See *A Concise Dictionary of Middle Egyptian*, p. 187.
2. From Arbeau, *Orchésographie*, ff. 45r–45v. In all translations from this work I have referred to the original French and also to the English editions by Beaumont and Evans.
3. Hogarth, *The Analysis of Beauty*, ed. Paulson, p. 103.
4. Ibid., p. 48.
5. Ibid., p. 103.
6. McGowan, *Dance in the Renaissance*, p. 198.
7. Translation adapted from *The Dialogues of Plato*, trans. Jowett, vol. 3, p. 726 (ref. 40c), and Francis Cornford, *Plato's Cosmology*, p. 135 (refs 40c and 40d). I am grateful for advice from M.A. Stewart.
8. Translation from Arbeau, *Orchésographie*, f. 104r.
9. Cited in Stevens, *Words and Music in the Middle Ages*, p. 179, from *The Apocryphal New Testament*, trans. M.R. James (Oxford: Clarendon Press, 1953), p. 253.
10. Cited in Robert Mullally, 'Reconstructing the *Carole*', p. 79.
11. The quotations are from authorized English translations of the original German editions. See Sachs, *World History of the Dance* (1963 reprint), pp. 10–11, and Köhler *The Mentality of Apes* (1927 edn), p. 314. For an exposé of Sachs's work, see Youngerman, 'Curt Sachs and his Heritage'.
12. Stravinsky, *An Autobiography*, p. 31.
13. From the translation by John Lydgate (*c.* 1430) of the verses from the Paris mural, as transcribed in Anon., *The Dance of Death*, ed. Florence Warren, p. 2, v. 2 (spelling modernized here).
14. *The Continuum Encyclopedia of Symbols*, p. 169.
15. *Hall's Dictionary of Subjects and Symbols in Art*, p. 291.
16. Forrest, *The History of Morris Dancing*, p. 74.
17. *The Poems of William Dunbar*, ed. Mackenzie (1990 reprint), no. 32, pp. 60–61.
18. Arena, *Ad suos Compagniones Studiantes*, trans. Guthrie and Zorzi, pp. 39–40.
19. *The Oxford Book of English Verse*, ed. Quiller-Couch, p. 729. I am grateful to Michael Wheeler for pointing out the connection.
20. Boccaccio, *The Decameron*, trans. McWilliam, p. 550.
21. Tennyson, *Poetical Works*, p. 48.
22. Hutton, *Stations of the Sun*, p. 234.

23. Arena, *Ad suos Compagniones Studiantes*, trans. Guthrie and Zorzi, p. 28.
24. Based on the similar and anonymous *S'ensuit l'art et instruction de bien dancer*.
25. Arena, *Ad suos Compagniones Studiantes*, trans. Guthrie and Zorzi, pp. 14, 30.
26. Hogarth, *The Analysis of Beauty*, ed. Paulson, p. 103.
27. Caroso, *Nobiltà di dame* (1600), trans. Sutton, p. 135.
28. Translated from Arbeau, *Orchésographie*, f. 25r.
29. Caroso, *Nobiltà di dame*, trans. Sutton, p. 96.
30. Hogarth, *The Analysis of Beauty*, ed. Paulson, p. 109.
31. Stanhope (Earl of Chesterfield), *Letters to his Son*, vol. 2, p. 76; letter dated 27 September 1748.
32. *Lowes' Ball-Conductor and Assembly Guide*, p. ii. The Lowe brothers, James, John, Joseph and Robert, leading dancing masters in Scotland during the first half of the nineteenth century, co-authored the book. See Lowe, *A New Most Excellent Dancing Master*, ed. Thomas, p. 5.
33. *The Encyclopædia of Dancing*, p. 83.
34. Gallini, *A Treatise on the Art of Dancing*, pp. 177–8.
35. *A Dictionary of Music and Musicians*, vol. 2, p. 45.
36. De Lauze, *Apologie de la Danse*, trans. Wildeblood, p. 83 (translation adapted).
37. *The Diary of Samuel Pepys*, ed. Latham and Matthews, vol. 3, pp. 300–301.
38. Wilson, *A Description of the Correct Method of Waltzing*, pp. xxxii, xxviii, xxix respectively.
39. Silvester, *This is Jive*, p. 11.
40. Ibid., p. 13.
41. Ibid., pp. 17–19.
42. Ibid., pp. 22–3.
43. Ibid., pp. 18–19.
44. Ebreo of Pesaro, *De pratica seu arte tripudii* (*On the Practice and Art of Dancing*), ed. and trans. Sparti, p. 91.
45. Smith, ed. and trans., *Fifteenth-Century Dance and Music*, vol. 1, p. 83. Cornazano's book was first written in 1455; a copy with the dedication quoted was made in about 1465.
46. Arena, *Ad suos Compagniones Studiantes*, trans. Guthrie and Zorzi, p. 9.
47. Arbeau, *Orchésographie*, f. 2v. Beaumont and Evans (see note 2) both translate 'l'espaule de mouton' (shoulder of mutton) as 'bad meat'.
48. De Lauze, *Apologie de la Danse*, trans. Wildeblood, p. 129.
49. Castiglione, *The Book of the Courtier*, trans. Hoby, p. 99; spelling modernized here.
50. Ibid., pp. 92–3; spelling modernized here.
51. Smith, ed. and trans., *Fifteenth-Century Dance and Music*, vol. 2, p. 204.
52. Cornazano, *The Book on the Art of Dancing*, trans. Inglehearn and Forsyth, p. 18. For an alternative translation, see Smith, ed. and trans., *Fifteenth-Century Dance and Music*, vol. 2, p. 85.

53. As cited in Scholes, *The Puritans and Music*, pp. 320–21.

54. As cited in Howard, *The Politics of Courtly Dancing*, p. 55.

55. Arbeau, *Orchésographie*, ff. 64v–65r.

56. See Tomlinson, *A Workbook by Kellom Tomlinson*, ed. Shennan, p. 92.

57. Cyril Rice, cited in Richardson, *A History of English Ballroom Dancing*, pp. 22–3.

58. Anon., *Solomon and Marcolf*, ed. and trans. Ziolkowski, p. 55.

59. Ibid., p. 53. Numbers at the start of sentences have been omitted.

60. From Newall, 'The Egg Dance', p. 35.

61. From the text to a copy of Sebald Beham's *Large Kermis*, trans. Stewart, in *Before Bruegel*, p. 158.

62. Arena, *Ad suos Compagniones Studiantes*, trans. Guthrie and Zorzi, p. 19.

63. Ibid., p. 20.

64. Auerbach, trans. Mannheim, *Literary Language and Its Public*, p. 37.

65. Gauchet, *Le plaisir des champs*, p. 65 (from the section 'La Feste', pp. 57–74). See McGowan, *Dance in the Renaissance*, pp. 202–7.

66. Mundy, *The Travels Of Peter Mundy*, ed. Temple, vol. 4, pp. 70–71; spelling and capitalization modernized here.

67. Egan, *Life in London*, p. 293.

68. Gronow, *Reminiscences*, vol. 1, pp. 31–3.

69. *International Encyclopedia of Dance*, vol. 6, p. 360.

70. Cellarius, *The Drawing-Room Dances*, p. 92. The waltz described occurs as a figure in a cotillon.

71. Byron, *The Works of Lord Byron*, vol. 9, p. 126.

72. Arbeau, *Orchésographie*, f. 24v.

73. Caroso, *Nobiltà di dame*, ed. and trans. Sutton, p. 146.

74. Arena, *Ad suos Compagniones Studiantes*, trans. Guthrie and Zorzi, p. 10.

75. Anon., *The Ball-room Guide*, p. 29.

76. Quirey, *May I Have the Pleasure?*, p. 66 (chapter title).

77. Anon., *The Ball-room Guide*, p. 26.

78. Ibid., p. 27.

79. Gronow, *Reminiscences*, vol. 2, pp. 297–8. According to Gronow, Lady Butler formed part of the set, along with the Countess of Jersey (see p. xx), that first performed the quadrille at Almack's in 1815.

80. Cellarius, *Fashionable Dancing*, p. 10.

81. Durang, *The Fashionable Dancer's Casket*, p. 24.

82. Anon., *The Ball-room Guide*, p. 24.

83. Richardson, *The Social Dances of the 19th Century*, p. 81.

84. Anon., *The Ball-room Guide*, p. 26.

85. Richardson, *The Social Dances of the 19th Century*, p. 118.

86. Stearns, *Jazz Dance*, p. 22.

87. Dannett and Rachel, *Down Memory Lane*, p. 65.

88. Stearns, *Jazz Dance*, p. 134.

89. Dannett and Rachel, *Down Memory Lane*, p. 65.

Select bibliography

REFERENCE WORKS AND WEBSITES

An American Ballroom Companion: Dance Instruction Manuals, Ca. 1490–1920 (Washington DC: Library of Congress), http://memory.loc.gov/ammem/dihtml/dihome.html; accessed 27 May 2011.

Catalogue of the Collection of Drawings in the Ashmolean Museum, Volume 1: *Netherlandish, German, French and Spanish Schools*, K.T. Parker (Oxford: Clarendon Press, 1938).

Catalogue of the Collection of Drawings in the Ashmolean Museum, Volume 4: *The Earlier British Drawings*, D.B. Brown (Oxford: Clarendon Press, 1982).

A Concise Dictionary of Middle Egyptian, Raymond O. Faulkner (Oxford: printed for the Griffith Institute at the University Press by Vivian Ridler, 1962).

The Continuum Encyclopedia of Symbols, Udo Becker, trans. Lance W. Garner (New York and London: Continuum, 2000).

A Dictionary of British Folk Customs, Christina Hole (London: Hutchinson, 1976; repr. London: Paladin, 1978).

A Dictionary of Music and Musicians, 4 vols, ed. Sir George Grove (London: Macmillan, 1879–89).

Dictionary of Subjects and Symbols in Art, James Hall (London: John Murray, 1974).

The Encyclopædia of Dancing, rev. edn, Chas. d'Albert (London: T.M. Middleton, n.d. [c. 1920]).

Illuminated Manuscripts in the Bodleian Library Oxford, Volume 1: *German, Dutch, Flemish, French, and Spanish Schools*, Otto Pächt and J.J.G. Alexander (Oxford: Clarendon Press, 1966).

Illuminated Manuscripts in the Bodleian Library Oxford, Volume 3: *British, Irish, and Icelandic Schools*, Otto Pächt and J.J.G. Alexander (Oxford: Clarendon Press, 1973).

International Encyclopedia of Dance, 6 vols (New York and London: Oxford University Press, 1998).

Oxford Art Online, www.oxfordartonline.com; accessed 27 May 2011.

Oxford Music Online (incl. *The New Grove Dictionary of Music and Musicians*), www.oxfordmusiconline.com; accessed 27 May 2011.

BOOKS AND ARTICLES

Adshead-Lansdale, Janet, and June Layson, *Dance History: An Introduction*, 2nd edn (London: Routledge, 1994).

Aldrich, Elizabeth, *From the Ballroom to Hell: Grace and Folly in Nineteenth-Century Dance* (Evanston IL: Northwestern University Press, 1991).

Anon., *The Ball-room Guide* (titled *The Ball Room Companion* on cover) (London: Frederick Warne, 1866).

Anon., *The Dance of Death*, ed. Florence Warren (London: Oxford University Press, for the Early English Text Society, 1931).

Anon., *S'ensuit l'art et instruction de bien dancer* (Paris: Michel Toulouze, n.d. [late fifteenth century]; facs. edn, London: Royal College of Physicians, 1936, and Geneva: Minkoff, 1985, under title *Dossier basses-dances*).

Anon., *S'ensuyvent plusieurs basses dances* (Lyon: Jacques Moderne, n.d. [c. 1532–3]; facs. edn, Geneva: Minkoff, 1985, under title *Dossier basses-dances*).

Anon., *Solomon and Marcolf*, parallel text, ed. and trans. from Latin, Jan M. Ziolkowski (Cambridge MA and London: Department of Classics, Harvard University, distributed by Harvard University Press, 2008).

Arbeau, Thoinot (pseudonym for Jehan Tabourot), *Orchésographie* (Langres: Jehan des Preyz, 1588, repr. 1589, 1596; facs. edn of 1596 repr. Geneva: Minkoff, 1972).

——, *Orchesography*, trans. Cyril Beaumont (London: Cyril W. Beaumont, 1925; repr. New York: Dance Horizons, 1968).

——, *Orchesography*, trans. Mary Stewart Evans (New York: Kamin Dance Publishers, 1948; repr. New York: Dover Publications, with a new Introduction and Notes by Julia Sutton, and a new Labanotation section by Mireille Backer and Julia Sutton, 1967).

Arena, Anthonius, *Ad suos Compagniones Studiantes* (n.p.: n. pub., 1529); parallel text, ed. and trans. John Guthrie and Marino Zorzi, as 'Rules of Dancing', with an introduction by Joan Rimmer, *Dance Research* (Edinburgh: Edinburgh University Press), vol. 4, no. 2 (1986), pp. 8–53.

Auerbach, Erich, *Literary Language and Its Public in Late Latin Antiquity and in the Middle Ages*, trans. Ralph Mannheim (New York: Pantheon, 1965).

Barlow, Jeremy, *The Cat & the Fiddle: Images of Musical Humour from the Middle Ages to Modern Times* (Oxford: Bodleian Library, 2006).

Boccaccio, Giovanni, *The Decameron*, trans. G.M. McWilliam, 2nd edn (London: Penguin Books, 1995).

Boswell, James, *Life of Johnson* (London: Oxford University Press, 1953, based on 3rd edn, 1799).

Brissenden, Alan, *Shakespeare and the Dance* (Highlands NJ: Humanities Press; repr. Alton: Dance Books, 2001).

Brown, Christopher, *Scenes of Everyday Life: Dutch Genre Paintings from the Mauritshuis* (Oxford: Ashmolean Museum, 1999).

Buckland, Theresa Jill, *Society Dancing: Fashionable Bodies in England 1870–1920* (Basingstoke: Palgrave Macmillan; New York: St Martin's Press, 2011).

Burden, Michael, and Jennifer Thorp, eds, *Dance & Image*, special issue of *Music in Art*, vol. 36, nos 1–2 (New York: Research Center for Music Iconography, CUNY, 2011).

Byron, Lord George, *The Works of Lord Byron*, 17 vols (London: John Murray, 1832–40).

Carner, Mosco, *The Waltz* (London: Max Parrish, 1948).

Caroso, Fabritio, *Il Ballarino* (Venice: Francesco Ziletti, 1581).

——, *Nobiltà di dame* (Venice: Muschio, 1600); ed. and trans. Julia Sutton (Oxford, New York: Oxford University Press, 1986).

Castiglione, Count Baldassare, *The Book of the Courtier*, trans. Sir Thomas Hoby (1561), with an Introduction by W.H.D. Rouse, and critical notes by W.B. Drayton Henderson (London: J.M. Dent, n.d. [*c*. 1928]).

Cawte, E.C., *Ritual Animal Disguise* (Cambridge: D.S. Brewer, 1978).

Cellarius, [Henri], *The Drawing-Room Dances* (London: E. Churton, 1847).

——, *Fashionable Dancing* (London: David Bogue, 1847).

Cornazano, Antonio: *The Book on the Art of Dancing*, trans. Madeleine Inglehearn and Peggy Forsyth (London: Dance Books, 1981).

Cornford, Francis, *Plato's Cosmology* (London: Kegan Paul, 1937).

Dannett, Sylvia G.L., and Frank R. Rachel, *Down Memory Lane: Arthur Murray's Picture Story of Social Dancing* (New York: Greenberg, 1954).

De Lauze, F[rançois], *Apologie de la Danse* (1623), parallel text, ed. and trans. Joan Wildeblood (London: Frederick Muller, 1952).

Dronke, Peter, *The Medieval Lyric*, 2nd edn (London: Hutchinson, 1978).

Dunbar, William, *The Poems of William Dunbar*, ed. W. Mackay Mackenzie, (London: Faber & Faber , 1932; repr. Edinburgh: James Thin, Mercat Press, 1990).

Durang, Charles, *The Fashionable Dancer's Casket, or the Ball-Room Instructor* (Philadelphia, Baltimore, New York, Boston MA: Fisher & Brother, n.d. [1856]).

Ebreo, Guglielmo, of Pesaro, *De pratica seu arte tripudii* (*On the Practice and Art of Dancing*) (1623), parallel text, ed. and trans. Barbara Sparti (Oxford: Clarendon Press, 1993).

Egan, Pierce: *Life in London* (London: Shirley, Neely, and Jones, 1821).

Forrest, John, *The History of Morris Dancing, 1458–1750* (Cambridge: James Clarke, 1999).

Gallini, Giovanni-Andrea, *A Treatise on the Art of Dancing* (London: Printed for the Author, 1762; repr. 1765, 1772).

Gauchet, Claude, *Le plaisir des champs* (Paris: Nicolas Chesnau, 1583).

Gronow, Captain (Rees Howell), *Reminiscences and Recollections*, 2 vols (London: J.C. Nimmo, 1892).

Grove, Lilly, et al., *Dancing* (London: Longmans, Green, 1907).

Heck, Thomas F., Robert Erenstein, M.A. Katritzky, Frank Peeters, A. William Smith and Lyckle de Vries, *Picturing Performance: The Iconography of the Performing Arts in Concept and Practice* (Rochester NY: University of Rochester Press, 1999).

Hogarth, William, *The Analysis of Beauty* (London: J. Reeves, 1753); ed. Ronald Paulson (New Haven CT and London: Yale University Press, 1997).

Howard, Skiles *The Politics of Courtly Dancing in Early Modern England* (Amherst: University of Massachusetts Press, 1998).

Hutton, Ronald, *Stations of the Sun* (Oxford: Oxford University Press, 1996).

Jonas, Gerald, *Dancing: The Power of Dance Around the World* (New York: Harry N. Abrams and London: BBC Books, 1992).

Köhler, Wolfgang, *The Mentality of Apes* (London: Kegan Paul, rev. and reset 1927, from 1925 edn); trans. Ella Winter from *Intelligensprüfungen am Menschenaffen* (Berlin: Julius Springer, 1917, rev. 1924 by author for translation).

Lindley, David, *Shakespeare and Music* (London: Thomson Learning (Arden Shakespeare), 2006).

Lowe [James, John, Joseph, Robert], *Lowes' Ball-Conductor and Assembly Guide* (Edinburgh: Messrs Lowe, n.d. [*c.*1820]).

Lowe, Joseph, *A New Most Excellent Dancing Master: The Journal of Joseph Lowe's visits to Balmoral and Windsor (1852–1860)*, ed. Allan Thomas (Stuyvesant NY: Pendragon Press, 1992).

McGowan, Margaret: *Dance in the Renaissance* (New Haven CT and London: Yale University Press, 2008).

Mullally, Robert, *The Carole: A Study of a Medieval Dance* (Aldershot: Ashgate, 2011).

——, 'Reconstructing the *Carole*', in *Reconstruction and Re-creation in Dance before 1850* (London: Proceedings of the fourth DHDS Conference, Dolmetsch Historical Dance Society, 2003).

Mundy, Peter, *The Travels Of Peter Mundy In Europe And Asia 1608–1667, Travels In Europe 1639–1647*, 5 vols, ed. Lt.-Col. Sir Richard Carnac Temple (London: Printed for the Hakluyt Society, 1907–36).

Nevile, Jennifer, ed., *Dance, Spectacle, and the Body Politick, 1250–1750* (Bloomington and Indianapolis: Indiana University Press, 2008).

Newall, Venetia, 'The Egg Dance', *Folk Music Journal* (London: English Folk Dance and Song Society), vol. 2, no. 1 (1970), pp. 35–44.

Pepys, Samuel, *The Diary of Samuel Pepys*, 11 vols, ed. Robert Latham and William Matthews (London: G. Bell, 1970–83).

Plato, *The Dialogues of Plato*, trans. Benjamin Jowett (Oxford: Clarendon Press, 1953).

Playford, John, and successors, *The Dancing Master*, 18 edns (London: John Playford, edns 1–7, 1651–1686, first edn title *The English Dancing Master*), (London: Henry Playford, edns 8–12, 1690–1703), (London: John Young, edns 13–18, 1706–*c.*1728, and also vol. 2, 4 edns, *c.*1713–28, and vol. 3, two issues, 1719 and *c.*1728).

Quiller-Couch, A.T., ed., *The Oxford Book of English Verse* (Oxford: Clarendon Press, 1900).

Quirey, Belinda, with Steve Bradshaw and Ronald Smedley, *May I Have the Pleasure? The Story of Popular Dancing* (London: BBC, 1976; repr. London: Dance Books, 1987 and 1993).

Reeser, Dr Eduard, *The History of the Waltz*, trans. W.A.G. Doyle-Davidson (Stockholm: Continental Book Company, n.d. [1949]).

Richardson, Philip J.S., *A History of English Ballroom Dancing (1910–1945)* (London: Herbert Jenkins, n.d. [1946]).

——, *The Social Dances of the 19th Century* (London: Herbert Jenkins, 1960).

Rogers, Ellis A., *The Quadrille: A Practical Guide to its Origin, Development and Performance* (Orpington: C. & E. Rogers, 2003).

Rust, Frances, *Dance in Society* (London: Routledge & Kegan Paul, 1969).

Sachs, Curt, *World History of the Dance* (New York: W.W. Norton, 1937; repr. 1963), trans. Bessie Schönberg from *Eine Weltgeschichte des Tanzes* (Berlin: Dietrich Reimer, Ernst Vohsen, 1933).

Scholes, Percy, *The Puritans and Music* (Oxford: Clarendon Press, 1934).

Seebass, Tilman, 'Iconography and Dance Research', *Yearbook for Traditional Music* (Canberra: International Council for Traditional Music), vol. 23 (1991), pp. 33–51.

Silvester, Victor, *Modern Ballroom Dancing* (London: Herbert Jenkins, 1927).

———, *This is Jive* (London: Danceland Publications, 1944).

Smith, A. William, ed. and trans., parallel text, *Fifteenth-Century Dance and Music: Twelve Transcribed Italian Treatises and Collections in the Tradition of Domenico da Piacenza*, 2 vols, (Stuyvesant NY: Pendragon Press, 1995).

Spencer, Peggy, *The Joy of Dancing* (London: André Deutsch, 1997; London: Carlton Books, 2004).

———, *The Joy of Dancing: The Next Steps* (London: André Deutsch, 1999; London: Carlton Books, 2005).

Stanhope, Philip Dormer (Earl of Chesterfield), *Letters to his Son*, 4 vols (London: J. Dodsley, 1774).

Stearns, Marshall and Jean, *Jazz Dance: The Story of American Vernacular Dance* (New York: Macmillan, 1968).

Stevens, John, *Words and Music in the Middle Ages* (Cambridge: Cambridge University Press, 1986).

Stewart, Alison, *Before Bruegel* (Aldershot: Ashgate, 2008).

Stravinsky, Igor, *An Autobiography* (New York: Simon & Schuster, 1936; repr. New York: W.W. Norton, 1962).

Tennyson, Alfred, *Poetical Works* (London: Oxford University Press, 1953).

Thompson, Allison, comp., *Dancing Through Time: Western Social Dance in Literature, 1400–1918* (Jefferson NC and London: McFarland, 1998).

Tomlinson, Kellom, *The Art of Dancing Explained by Reading and Figures* (London: Printed for the Author, 1735).

———, *A Workbook by Kellom Tomlinson* (1708), ed. Jennifer Shennan (Stuyvesant NY: Pendragon Press, 1992).

Wilson, Thomas, *A Description of the Correct Method of Waltzing, the Truly Fashionable Species of Dancing* (London: Sherwood, Neely, and Jones, 1816).

Youngerman, Suzanne, 'Curt Sachs and his Heritage: A Critical Review of *World History of the Dance*, with a Survey of Recent Studies That Perpetuate his Ideas', *CORD News* (New York: Committee on Research in Dance), vol. 6, no. 2 (July 1974), pp. 6–19.

Illustrations and sources

The location of prints and drawings in the Ashmolean are identified by reference to numbering in the catalogues by D.B. Brown or K.T. Parker listed in the Bibliography, unless they are from uncatalogued material in the Douce Collection, in which case the Douce Box references are given.

Index

Page references to illustrations are in italic